Praise for JAVA

"The greatest gift from Sage's workshop was realizing that helping my dog with his issues, I'm helping me with mine."
~ **Christine MacGillivray, Canine Guardian**

"Out of all the powerful things I learned from you and Java, one thing stands out: mindfulness. You've shown me another level."
~ **Liz Tufte, Canine/Feline/Equine Guardian**

"Your dedication to Java and her progress has been heartwarming to witness!"
~ **Kathy Cascade, Tellington TTouch® Instructor**

"You are such an amazing teacher, Sage. I really appreciate that you are so exacting, that you are a thoughtful observer, and that your tender heart spills out all over the place. I recommend Tellington TTouch® and you to everyone I know with animals."
~ **Judy Williamson, Canine Guardian**

"The biggest lesson I learned in Sage's workshop is that you and your dog are an extension of each other."
~ **Jim Hermann, Canine Guardian**

"Thanks so much, Sage, for all you taught us. We are blessed." ~ **Deb Vadnais, Canine Guardian**

"Sage's TTouch workshop allowed me to observe my dog, Viva, with new eyes, and myself with new eyes, too. It has completely changed the way I relate to both animals and people."
~ **Kathryn Ananda-Owens, Canine/Feline Guardian**

"Sage's workshop made my heart ring! I want more!"
~ **Candi Storm, Feline/Equine Guardian**

I

"LIFE IS EITHER
A DARING ADVENTURE
OR NOTHING."
- HELEN KELLER

JAVA

THE TRUE STORY OF A SHELTER DOG WHO RESCUED A WOMAN

SAGE LEWIS

Published by Dancing Porcupine LLC
303 East Gurley Street #121
Prescott, AZ 86301

For more information:
www.DancingPorcupine.com

All rights reserved.
No part of this book may be reproduced,
scanned, or distributed in any printed or electronic form
without permission from the author.

Photography: Copyright © 2006 by Allen Brown
https://AllenBrownPhotography.com

Design: Sage Lewis

First Edition © 2006
Second Edition © 2015
Third Edition © 2019

ISBN 978-0-578-53875-4

THE TRUE STORY OF A SHELTER DOG

WHO RESCUED A WOMAN

~ THIRD EDITION ~

SAGE LEWIS

© 2019 Dancing Porcupine LLC

JAVA 11/2/00-3/2/13

You touched every cell in my being.
Thank you, Boom!

For my Little Brown Bear, Java.

*Thank you for teaching me to open my heart —
to risk running free and truly living
rather than dying old and bored.*

*And for all of the animals and humans who have been
misunderstood at some point in their lives.*

You are the greatest teachers.

TABLE OF CONTENTS

1: LOVE *Boing, Kaboing, Sproing!*   1

2: FEAR *Whale Eyes & Butterflies*   15

3: ANGER *In Complete Out of Control*   29

4: PATIENCE *In & Out of the Canyon*   49

5: AWARENESS *Spiritual Warrior Princess*   75

6: UNDERSTANDING *Angel Pie*   85

7: GRATITUDE *Selling Bananas to Monkeys*   109

8: RESPECT *Do I Have To Stop?*   125

9: TRUST *The Birth of a Porcupine*   137

10: CHANGE *Sea Green Eyes & Willow Trees*   149

11: PEACE *From the Plott Hound's Mouth*   169

12: GROWTH *Unlocking the Inner Door*   179

13: FAITH *Python Lifts & Emotional Shifts*   201

14: LETTING GO *Pebbles, Rocks & Gemstones*   221

15: FREEDOM *Becoming a Creature Teacher*   277

16: BALANCE *Coming Full Circle & a Quarter*   237

THE TAIL END   247

THE AUTHORS   249

TELLINGTON TTOUCH®   251

FOREWORD

By Edie Jane Eaton and Linda Tellington-Jones

Sage and Java bounced their way eagerly into my five-day Tellington TTouch® Training in Minneapolis, Minnesota during the spring of 2002. I noticed them right away—an enthusiastic pair with a strong connection to one another. Java, a well-muscled dog with a glossy coat of brown and tan tiger stripes, was the first Plott Hound I had ever met, and also the first time I'd ever heard of the breed. "Plott" may sound like "plod", but there was *nothing* plodding about Java!

She was very expressive in a lot of energetic ways, and was lucky to be with a human, not only with the perceptiveness of Sage, but also with the energy to keep up with her and guide her. Sage was very open to helping Java succeed— flexible and willing to try the myriad of new ideas and tools the TTouch work presented. Helping Java find a comfortable and peaceful place within herself became Sage's priority, and she never wavered from this commitment.

Over the course of the next year and a half, I had the opportunity to instruct three more of Java and Sage's TTouch Trainings, and their growth and change was a beautiful dance to observe. I saw Sage and Java becoming closer at the same time that Java's own sense of self and poise increased.

Java's ability to be comfortable within a group of dogs changed dramatically during this time, and, all the while, Sage was making sure that the path she was on was Java's path and not her own. She always put Java's needs first, and provided her with a safe and loving environment within which to blossom.

This book is a lovely tribute to Tellington TTouch®, a method that works so profoundly to change the way animals feel about themselves. Through this work we learn to be nonjudgmental, neutral, open, and to recognize that there's always a possibility for change in all beings.

JAVA: The True Story of a Shelter Dog Who Rescued a Woman will go straight to the heart of those who are committed to all animals, and especially those who have spent time with difficult ones.

With love,
Edie Jane Eaton

Edie Jane's fascination with the Feldenkrais Method —the principles of which underlie the TTEAM & TTouch work—led her to become a Feldenkrais Practitioner. She also travels the world as a TTEAM and TTouch Instructor. When not traveling and teaching, Edie Jane keeps busy with her private TTouch and Feldenkrais practice and workshops, and delights in being at home with her friends, family and garden.
www.listeningtowhispers.com

By Linda Tellington-Jones

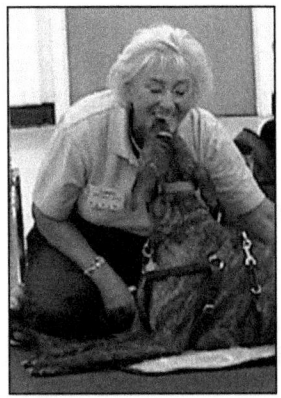

As I walked into the facility on the first day of that TTouch graduation during the fall of 2003, I scanned the room. A tall, lean, dark-haired woman stood before me with a big smile and a gorgeous brown and tan striped creature wagging hesitantly at her side. They both caught my eye and heart and I instantly wanted to know them better.

I knew nothing of Sage and Java's past. Greeting them both as they were, I saw a pair of beautiful, eager beings who adored one another, yet both seemed held back by their fears. Sage appeared to be a very concerned "doggie mama" whose past experiences were causing her to hold on to how Java acted in the past. Yet behind those sea green eyes I saw so much love and concern for not only Java's well-being, but also the other beings in the room. Sage was a vivacious, highly intelligent, curious woman whose soul exuded extreme love, compassion and honesty.

Java came across to me as a beautiful, whimsical dog who hadn't had enough chance for socialization. She was eager but reactive, and seemed very connected to Sage—picking up on Sage's fears and lack of trust—and feeling uncertain about her own choices.

Since that first meeting years ago, the changes between Sage and Java have been totally delightful to watch unfold. What a step-by-step journey of discovery the two of them have made—hand in paw, so to speak. As Sage gained trust in Java, a humorous side to them both took wings—a side that now allows them to soar together. I love the enthusiasm I saw in both of them the last time—the utter joy, trust and confidence that blossomed over time.

JAVA: The True Story of a Shelter Dog Who Rescued a Woman is a loving example of honesty, insights and self-examination. Through this book, you will find hope and magic for your own lives as Sage's words unfold the beautiful yet challenging reality of working with animals and working with yourself.

I so greatly appreciate the gifts both Sage and Java have given by sharing their journey with others. You will, too.

Aloha,
Linda Tellington-Jones

Linda Tellington-Jones founded the Tellington Touch Equine Awareness Method (TTEAM) in 1975 and became a Feldenkrais Practitioner in 1978. In 1983, Linda founded the Tellington TTouch for Companion Animals, followed by the beginnings of Tellington TTouch for Humans research. Linda has given many TTouch demonstrations, most notably to the American Holistic Veterinary Association, German Veterinary Association, various veterinary schools in Germany and Switzerland, the University of California School of Veterinary Medicine, University of Minnesota School of Veterinary Medicine, and American Humane Society of the United States. Linda shares her life in Hawaii with her husband, Roland Kleger.

DEDICATION

There aren't enough words to fully express my gratitude for three beings in my life who have helped to make me more of who I am today. They have taught me how to reach for the stars and take time to stop and smell the moments along the way. Two are human—the other, a canine. Allen Brown was my main lifeline during the early process of this book and he supported me mentally, physically, emotionally, and spiritually for many years. I am so grateful for having him in my life (and for being our photographer!) and for loving Java as much as I did. That's no simple task! We continue to be wonderful friends.

The second human is my husband, James Schattauer. He picked up in our lives a few years after this book left off. James had the great fortune of being with Java in her later years - from age 7 through her aging and passing journey. It's because of James that Java got to run free on a private island and also ran free for many consecutive summers on 360 private acres in Southern Wisconsin. James clearly loved Java as much as I did and vice versa. We both still miss Java greatly.

Then there's Java aka "The Boom!" Without her, this book wouldn't have been possible. The first printing of this book in 2006 made its way around the world and her story has touched thousands of lives since. Java provided me with 12-1/2 amazing years of life lessons and unconditional love and companionship. She brought me back to the moment on a daily basis, and made me laugh with her animated antics and whimsical spirit.

When I worked too hard, she pressed her head on my arm and dropped a toy in my lap, looked sideways, wagged her tail and grumbled at me. When I was upset, she'd find me, lick my tears away, and usually ended up lying on top of me until I burst out laughing. When I was happy, she joined in on the happy parade and we danced, laughed, and played freely together. Java stood by my side through my divorce, the beginnings and endings of relationships, two career changes, moving three times, the death of my father, the death of two canine companions, depression, anxiety, love, change, and growth. Java is the reason I do the work I do with animals. She taught me that to love freely and unconditionally is a necessity, and that it actually *is* possible in humans, too.

Thank you, you three. I have learned to open my heart more than I ever knew possible.

Love and gratitude,
Sage

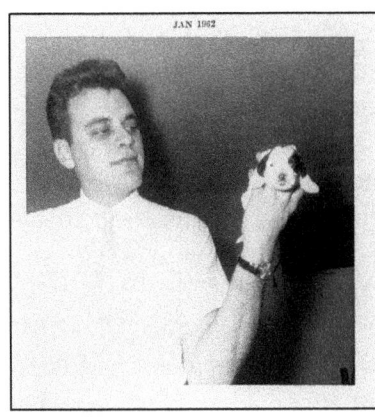

THANKS

It is with deepest gratitude that I thank the following people and animals for making such a big impact on my life, and giving me the courage and material to write this book.

First of all, a huge hug to my sister, Stephanie Frank; thank you for kicking me in the butt, cheering, crying, laughing, helping me make my words make sense, and reminding me to also market myself instead of just making things look pretty.

Another huge thank you to my Mom, Karen Lewis; thank you for having me, supporting me, loving me, and encouraging absolutely everything I've ever set out to do in my life—including my dream of finding a way to make money by petting animals.

A big, belly hug for my Dad, Michael Lewis; thank you for still finding your way into my dreams at night, and for being my guardian angel during the day; for inspiring me, loving me, accepting me, dancing with me and making me laugh; and for teaching me to go after what feels right—even if it sounds as crazy as selling hot dogs on the beach.

XVII

Thank you to all of the incredible animals I've had the opportunity to meet, work with, and learn from over the years. You continue to be my greatest teachers.

To my beautiful therapist friend, Joan; thank you for telling me years ago that a book waited to be written from inside me. You were right.

A heartfelt thank you to my entire Tellington TTouch® family for holding Java's leash(es) and my hand and heart over the years. Your continued love and support are what kept us going.

Thank you to all of the wonderful people who have passed through my life—or stayed awhile—and for supporting, encouraging, and being bold enough to play with both Java and I. You know who you are.

Lastly, I'd like to give a huge thank you to Rebecca Mataya. Thank you for asking me to go with you to rescue a bouncy, brindle pup from the shelter that day.

And for lending me forty bucks to pay for her.

PREFACE

I remember it as if it were yesterday. Dressed to look like the sweet, little girl I was, I felt unbelievably proud of being chosen. At age five there was nothing better than kindergarten. There we were, a bunch of giggly, wiggly little children lined up like individual crayons on the floor, lying impatiently on our primary-colored mats.

We pretended to take a nap, but in reality, we were just waiting for that special moment. Struggling to settle my body, I heard the clickety-clack of my teacher's navy-blue heels on the linoleum floor, and I giggled in anticipation.

As the clickety-clack came to a halt by my head, a warm hand reached down to touch my arm. Finally, it was my turn! Handing me the magic wand with a silver tinfoil star on top, I was the chosen one. My mission? Wake up the kids one at a time by gently touching them on the shoulder with the wand.

Unfortunately, I was overzealous, even at age five. Walking proudly through the sea of squirmy children, I began to wake up my classmates with my special, super powers. Then, I lost my balance. My clunky, red, orthopedic shoe found its way quickly onto a finger, which was attached to a hand, which was attached to one of my classmates. A high-pitched, girl-squeal filled the air like a siren as I stumbled to catch myself.

It was an accident!
It was an accident!

But through the tiny giggles of my classmates the teacher gently asked that I put my wand away and sit down. My sister did the same thing a few years earlier but she whacked all the kids on the head. It must run in the family. Born pigheaded, I never quite gave up the idea that I had special powers. I've held that magic wand close to my heart since then, even though I was asked to put it away when I was five.

Not always one to follow the rules or take the same path as everyone else, somehow I always get where I want to be. In one, powerful, nap-waking moment, I realized the power of holding the wand, and that the choices I made in life were mine — and sometimes there are challenges and consequences.

One of those challenges was the Grand Canyon. On the day before my hike into the Big Hole, I met with a psychic in Sedona, Arizona. Victor informed me I would be challenged repeatedly in my lifetime. I felt both invigorated and worried.

Having already spent fourteen years in a tumultuous marriage, surviving a serious car accident, and a recent divorce, I faced a hike into the Grand Canyon the next day. What could possibly be more challenging than what I'd already experienced? Feeling angry, scared and excited all at the same time, I tucked his information away for later.

Victor's words rang clear to me that day, when he told me, "You have an incredible amount to offer to the world, and you will be challenged over and over again."

He was right. Challenged I've been, and offered I've done. It's my pleasure to share with you the light, dark and everything in between of my journey from then to now. I never dreamed I'd be where I am today—writing, creating, teaching, working with people and animals, and loving life. There isn't any reason for why my life has gone the way it has, other than it's the way it's supposed to be.

Years ago, my therapist told me that resiliency holds a special gift for those brave enough to tackle it. I figured resiliency was just a necessary part of life that everyone experienced if they wanted to survive the challenges of living.

Challenges? We all have them. I've experienced my share of challenges, as I'm sure you have, too. It is because of the challenges my life presented me that I'm able to share my lessons with you. I look at challenges as opportunities—as beautiful gems that teach us how to grow and change, rather than obstacles that keep us stuck in fear. It doesn't mean that on some days I haven't wanted to whip those stupid gems back into the river and scream at my Higher Power for all of the blessed challenges. I've done that, too. But the lessons I've learned along the way, by choosing to see obstacles as opportunities, have made me who I am—just as your challenges have molded your life and experiences.

Java's story gently nudged me, and sometimes snarled at me, to write this book and share both of our stories. The dance we shared together for 12-1/2 years reflects the dualism in our lives in a way that's creepy, clumsy, and filled with absolute stunning beauty. She's my angel, and I know I was hers.

It is my sincere wish to you that you learn, enjoy, and live your life the way you truly want to live. With each new day, may you walk your path with awareness and love—knowing you have the power to wave your own sparkly, magic wand.

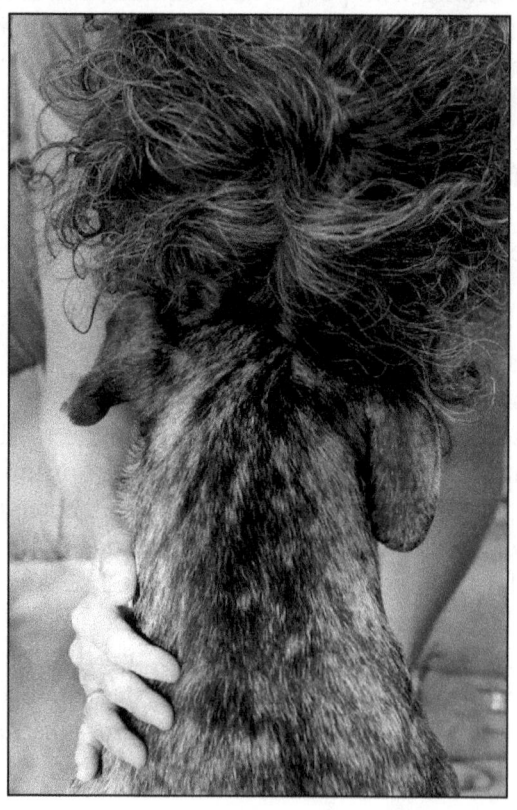

SAGE & JAVA – SUMMER 2012
Photo Credit ® 2012: www.GinaEasley.com

CHAPTER ONE

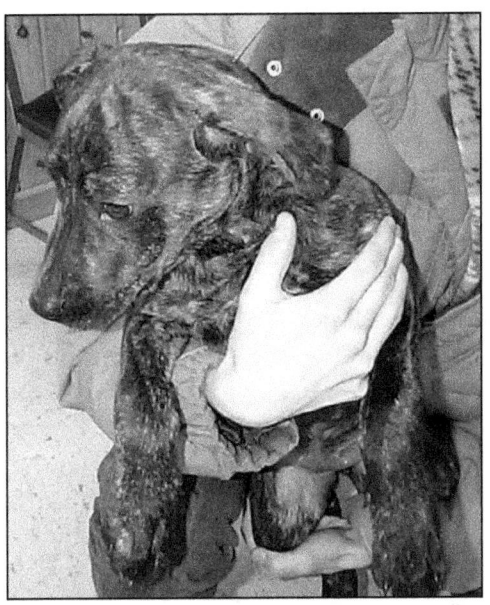

LOVE

"The best and most beautiful things in the world cannot be seen or even touched — they must be felt with the heart."
~ Helen Keller

I believe in love at first sight. There's something about that instantaneous feeling. It grabs every cell in your body, and makes you feel as if something immediately shifts inside you. If you're lucky enough, the other being feels it, too. Like a rocket blasting off, there's a heat and energy that only some of us can describe in words, yet the feeling in our hearts is crystal clear. I once read that it's only in the heart where anything really happens. Love is lucky to live there.

The first moment I laid eyes on her, my whole soul shifted to a place that was like a dream. I was floating gracefully on a pink, fluffy cloud as everything downshifted into slow motion—except her. My life was going to change. I could feel it. How dramatically it would change, I didn't know. Thank goodness I was naive or she would have stayed at the shelter that morning.

Have you ever walked into an animal shelter and connected deeply with one specific animal? So deeply you felt your heart become wider and freer, and chills ran up and down your spine? You walk slowly down the rows and rows of bleach-scented caged runs, and there's almost always one special being who pulls gently, or sometimes demandingly, at your heartstrings. If you're like me, there's *always* one.

Maybe it's the shaggy, quiet one lying in the back of the kennel, looking sheepishly yet lovingly straight into your eyes through the scraggled fur that's covering theirs. Or maybe it's the other one, two doors down—the one who wags its whole body feverishly and smiles along with you as you pass by. You keep going, but then you can't help yourself so you back up to take a second look. For some of you, like me, it's the one you can't explain in words because only your heart knows the real answer.

I happened to be sitting at home on that blustery, winter morning in February of 2001—the year I perfectly deemed *The Year of Love*. On the other side of town, my soon-to-be ex-husband was gathering up his last load of stuff that he wanted and I didn't—hauling it away from the life we built together for over fourteen years. I still felt kind of scared and a bit wobbly in my new role as a single woman. Actually, I felt really scared and very wobbly. I had moved out on my own only a few months earlier, taking my dog, Clio, my car, and my heart, (along with a few material items like clothes and the furniture that was light and easy to carry). Our world seemed very small, just Clio and I, so I adopted a second senior greyhound, Veta, a week after we had our own house. I landed softly in a very fragile, new place, and now my life was about to change.

As I gazed sleepily out the front picture window of my grey love shack, small white flakes of new snow began to drift and swirl their way into my vision. Losing myself in a trance of miniature dancing snowflakes, I startled quickly when the phone rang. My phone didn't ring very often, and I wondered who was calling so early on a Saturday morning.

My one senior greyhound, Clio, lifted her head briefly from its resting point on the turquoise blue, velvet pillow on her side of the throne, while my other senior greyhound, Veta, peered sideways at me from the opposite end. World's fastest couch potatoes. I laughed at my hound bookends lying gracefully with their needle-nose heads on my velvet pillows as I walked to answer the phone.

"Hello, this is Sage," I said hesitantly—wondering who or what I might hear in response. It was my friend, Rebecca.

"What are you doing right now?" she asked quickly enough that I knew she was up to something fun, or no good.

Rebecca and I had volunteered together with Wisconsin Greyhound Pets of America for a few years. Her call came to see if I wanted to take a short road trip to the Iowa County Humane Society in Dodgeville, Wisconsin to rescue a pup.

"They think she's a greyhound—a twelve-week-old, brindle, female. You wanna go get her with me?" she asked with excitement.

My mind didn't even flutter, but my heart sure did.

"YES!"

Without much thought, I threw on my bright orange, way-too-puffy winter coat, kissed Clio and Veta goodbye, and scurried to the curb to wait for her cherry red mini-van to peek around the corner. Minutes later, Rebecca and her chariot arrived, and the path I headed down in that moment brought a huge adrenaline rush. My gut said I might come home with a puppy, while my mind and heart prepared to duke it out.

Shutting the car door, I squirmed in my seat, then squealed like a little kid waiting in a long line to ride the roller coaster that had not one, but TWO, huge corkscrews,

"Is she spoken for yet?" I asked impatiently.

"Nope," Rebecca paused briefly, "We'll get her into a foster home this afternoon," she said coyly—glancing sideways at me with a huge smile, "unless you want her," she grinned.

It felt all too perfect. I lived only two blocks from the school where I worked as an elementary art instructor, and owned a house with a large fenced yard. There was no one in my life anymore to approve or disapprove of a puppy, except me.

My mind danced like a squirrel on a trampoline as I realized that this opportunity might never present itself again in my lifetime. If I wanted to come home with a puppy, I could.

Did I want to? Maybe.

I always wanted a greyhound puppy and to find one at a shelter was unheard of, but the closer we got to the shelter, the more my mind raced with wonder and worry.

Did I even remember what it was like to have a puppy?
Did I know what to do with one?
What color collar should I buy this afternoon?

It's interesting what happens when your heart is the main part involved in a decision. Your head takes a back seat. We ended up at a rural, no-kill shelter about forty miles southwest of Madison, Wisconsin. Adjoining the shelter was a paint ball facility and a taxidermy place. Interesting combination. I peered through the window and was startled by the images that stared back at me. Big, glassy, deer eyeballs watched me closely from the part of their body that jutted out from the wall.

I wondered briefly what I was getting myself into, but when the chorus of barks rang out from behind the door, my wonder turned to excitement. The director of the shelter walked toward our two smiling heads at the glass door, welcomed us in, then locked it behind him.

"You're just in time," the director said as he unlocked the door of opportunity.

Rebecca was on good terms with him, and he didn't want to adopt the pup out until it was decided if Wisconsin Greyhound Pets of America should take her or not. The shelter opened to the public in an hour, which meant she'd be up for adoption. I never knew how precious this timing was until I looked back on it a few months later. An hour can make a world of difference.

"She's a cute pup and I think she's a greyhound. Her name is Maddie, or Madison. Why don't you check her out and see what you think? She came in a week ago so her quarantine is up today," the director told Rebecca as he led us into the dog area.

At this point, the Universe began throwing Cupid's arrows toward me and pointing at neon signs that read,

"Take the puppy! NOW!"

There's this thing that takes place where you can divide your senses into little parcels. It's like walking into a bakery and you smell the goods long before you see and hear. You can almost taste what's hiding underneath the glass counters, waiting for you to take it home to enjoy one sensuous bite at a time. Or, maybe you can't wait to get in the car to devour the delicious pastry on the way home. Life goes one frame at a time sometimes.

I'll never forget the first moment I laid eyes on her from the opposite end of the cement pathway that connected us. Like a red carpet rolled out for a queen to parade across, the distance between us shortened as we readied ourselves to meet for the very first time. I slowly passed the rows of chain link kennel doors, while scents I'd rather not describe quickly invaded my nostrils. My senses were heightened—pinpointing each scent, sound, and sight as individual little morsels of knowledge.

A tiny, brown blur, Maddie scurried frantically back and forth on the cement with a mixture of joy and uncertainty—happy to be freed from her kennel. Like a single frame pulled from a full feature movie reel, Maddie popped clearly into my vision during a moment of stillness. I grinned.

This stocky little puppy looked nothing like a greyhound, but rather a cartoonish cross between a greyhound and a pit bull terrier. And by the worried look in her eyes and the tenseness in her body, she appeared to me as the most skittish puppy I had seen before.

Having lived peacefully with greyhounds for ten years, this squirmy pup seemed somewhat intriguing to someone like me who spent most of her time with easy, lazy couch potatoes. Back then, I thought all greyhounds were lazy and quiet, and all other breeds were otherwise. What did I know? I've since learned that it's not always the case.

Like a tall, alien creature struggling through molasses, I moved in slowly and came closer to Maddie's space. Catching another quick glimpse of her true self, Maddie whizzed past me on her pogo stick legs. And then she bounced back toward me. Bending over, I reached out my hand toward her tiny, energetic frame—something I'd never do today knowing how scary that can be for many dogs. In a fleeting moment, Maddie ran quickly away from me, then back with the same intensity and speed. Her dark, brindle coloring created a stunning, mosaic pattern of yin and yang, as darkness intertwined with lightness. Her small, muscular body was rubbery yet dense, and as she wiggled to and fro, her little spirit began filling the entire room with love.

"What do you think?" asked the shelter director, as his eyes followed Maddie's bouncing body across the floor.

"Well, we're not sure, but we've got a foster home for her this afternoon, so we'll take her just in case she truly *is* a greyhound," Rebecca replied, then looked at me and grinned.

We both knew better.

The shelter director scooped spastic, little Maddie up into his arms, and as she squirmed with wide eyes, he carried her into the front lobby and stuck her in a small, fenced playpen. With front legs, back legs, head, ears and tail going in opposite directions, this pup jumped higher than I knew was possible from a small being.

Peering over at Rebecca, I chuckled nervously, "With a vertical jump like hers, we should name her Pogo."

Standing at the front desk, I caught a repetitive motion out of the corner of my eye, as Maddie's out-of-control body jumped up and down, up and down, up and down, while I tried my hardest to listen to *why* she was surrendered to the shelter.

Somewhere amidst the conversation, I overheard that the man who brought Maddie to the shelter said he found her on the side of the road. There was very little background information on her.

Boing, Kaboing, Sproing!

As I detected more motion from my peripheral vision, anxiety rose in my belly. Finally, I couldn't watch anymore. Over the fence I went, and in mid-jump, I scooped Maddie up under her armpits and curled the little stress ball up to my orange, puffy coat. Complete utter stillness. Maddie and I both let out a huge sigh of relief, relaxed our bodies, and looked deeply into each other's eyes for the first time. That was all it took for us to fall madly in love with one another—touch.

Rebecca wrote a check for forty dollars to spring the pup from the shelter, while I inhaled puppy breath deeply into my lungs. With Maddie comfortably in my arms, the three of us headed back to the van for the ride home.

Rebecca and I looked at one another in silence, then glanced down at Maddie who had already curled up into a tiny, little ball on my lap and fallen sound asleep. She was snoring within moments—something years later I wished she would grow out of, but hasn't. I was amazed at how small her body looked, and was mesmerized by her complete solitude after all of the boinging and sproinging I'd witnessed.

During the ride home, my head decided to steer the ship.

What on earth was I thinking?
Was I capable of taking on this responsibility?
Would my other two senior greyhounds get along with her?
How would I feel if she went to a foster home?
For goodness sake, she's not a Maddie!

By the time we drove a mile away from the shelter, my heart shifted into first gear and passed my head as the decision maker. If Maddie got along well with my other two dogs, she'd stay. Thank goodness I didn't know then what I know now. A big, personal, thank you to my own naiveté for a lot of the happenings in my life—especially this one.

When you're truly in love, the whole world goes away and nothing else matters. Rebecca and I came to a halt in front of my house, then we headed up the walkway with an air of confidence.

Maddie's dense, little body relaxed in my arms as I fumbled in my pocket for the key. In hindsight, it never dawned on me there was a possibility things *wouldn't* work out this well. As I unlocked the door, Veta and Clio greeted us in the entry, then sniffed the contents in my arms. I plopped Maddie onto the floor and informed them we were increasing the size of our family by one. One puppy.

"HERE!" I said, as Maddie stood lazily before them, wagging her tail.

The merry-go-round of butt sniffing began as they sniffed and wagged like they'd been waiting for her arrival forever. Then the three of them followed one another in a precise single file line to go potty together outside. Looking around sheepishly, Maddie waddled clumsily into the middle of the back yard, hunched her back and lifted her tail. She looked over at me with a combination of concern and relief in her eyes, as my mouth popped wide open in awe. The expanse of what came next will be etched in my mind forever, and now yours.

"My God! She pooped the size of a ROPE!!" Rebecca laughed uncontrollably, as Maddie finished creating her gigantic monument in the yard.

I couldn't help laughing, too. It *was* funny—and impressive. It appeared that the poor, little thing waited to potty for a week, and what came out of her was half her weight in waste. She looked much skinnier now than at the shelter, as she squealed around the yard with pride and ease. Veta, Clio, Rebecca and I watched with joy as Maddie sniffed every inch of her new yard, then bounded through the air like a gazelle who just won the lottery. It was then that I first saw the shift from fear to happiness transform Maddie's sweet, little face and I smiled deeply with love. Veta and Clio trotted gracefully to the back door, as Maddie blazed a trail to follow, then skidded clumsily to a halt. Opening the sliding, glass door, I watched the parade of dogs enter our home together for the first time, and felt very outnumbered. The parade turned quickly into a siesta as Veta, Clio and Maddie snuggled up in the living room—all three in the same bed together. I guess it was going to be okay!

Rebecca and I stared at Maddie like two giddy old ladies at a flea market, as Maddie stared back at us—a puppy, waiting to play. Taking in every little nuance of her being, we finally decided to give in and toss a ball. Spinning, bouncing, running, more spinning, diving—Maddie chased the ball and brought it back for more. Smart puppy.

A short while later, a knock at the door signaled the foster family ready to pick up Maddie. Almost before we even said hello, I blurted out how Maddie had already become a part of my family the moment she walked in the door, if not before. Maddie skidded to a halt at their feet, and then chased her tail around, and around—stopping long enough for them to see her fiery eyes and mischievous smile. They seemed quite relieved to leave empty handed, and smiled graciously as they watched Maddie bounce off the walls of *my* house instead of *theirs*.

When things slowed down a bit, and the energy shifted, I was able to look at her. I mean *really* look and truly *see* her. Maddie's eyes were the most stunning reddish-brown, like the rich, warm color of a polished chestnut glistening in the sunlight. Full of expression, depth, and secret experiences, the depth in her eyes went straight to my heart, as the innocence in her eyes reflected back toward me. Like two turn signals atop her head, Maddie's velvety soft ears sat crooked yet alert, with her right one creased in half and sticking out like it was directing traffic, and her left one lying flat and behaving. Her short, black eyelashes sat in a perfectly spaced row and her muzzle was square, broad, and well-defined.

Her teeth were like sharp, little razors that juxtaposed the light, pink tongue that rested between them. Her neck was long and lean, and as she sat facing me, I noticed six, tan and dark brown cowlicks in a perfect row across the front of her chest. She flopped over onto her side to test her cute, puppy meter, and I smiled at the dark marking smack dab in the middle of her chest. A heart. Her legs were strong and firm, and by the size of her paws I wondered how big she'd get. Her tiny toenails were more like sharp fir tree needles yet they were decorated with tan and black stripes, and the pads on her feet were as smooth as glass. I found myself mesmerized by the myriad of colors that created her fur, as shades and tints of every color brown imaginable weaved in and out across her entire body. Looking at me out of the side of her eyes, her pointy, rubbery tail was wagging non-stop.

"I love you," I said to Maddie, as she cocked her head to the right as if to pay closer attention.

Those first few hours together, Maddie seldom seemed to stop moving unless I picked her up and held her closely against my heart. Whether it was her idea or mine, we cuddled a lot from the very beginning because it felt so nice to both of us. There's nothing better than snuggling with a puppy when you're healing from heartache—or even when you're not.

With the news spreading fast, more knocks came at the door, as a few friends stopped by to see my new arrival later in the day. I was surprised to notice that when people reached toward her, Maddie ran quickly away from them, and then buried her tense body in mine. Within only a few short hours together, Maddie had come to trust me, and allowed me to see that she was quite anxious around new people. I could already sense that I had my hands full. If I had been wiser at the time, I would have waited a few days for the grooming marathon that came next, but I figured that having extra hands would get the job done more quickly. Sometimes intention is stronger than paying attention, and not necessarily better.

While one friend held Maddie, I grabbed a nail clipper and quickly dulled her eighteen weapons. Next, we hauled her squirmy body to the tub for two consecutive baths — quickly removing the week-long kennel stench from her dull, dry, and brittle coat. After a few hours of marveling at how beautiful Maddie looked, felt and smelled, my friends congratulated me on my new acquisition, then wished us well on our adventure as they walked out the door. Veta and Clio sighed from atop the couch.

The energy in my house quickly transformed from chaos to solitude, as I sat alone in my yellow, flowery reading chair and looked out my front window. Naked branches bounced lightly among the winter trees, as the crescent moon peeked out to say hello. The sky was beginning to dim its lights for the night, as shadows danced playfully across the blanket of snow in my yard. With all three dogs sound asleep together, I let out a strong exhale of puppy love, then closed my eyes from exhaustion. As I drifted off to a colorful slumber, the sound of the telephone jostled me from a dream. Two rings later, I walked slowly to pick it up, as Maddie shook herself vigorously from sleep, then followed closely at my heels.

"Hello?" I answered slowly in a tired daze.

A familiar inhale on the other end of the line tugged at my heart. My soon-to-be ex-husband was calling in tears as he left our house in Madison with his last truckload of material stuff.

"It's me," he said quietly, then paused his soft and gentle voice to catch his breath. "Sage, I want you to know that I really love you."

My heart filled with lightness as a lengthy pause filled the air. Smiling deeply inside, I remembered fondly how easy it had been to love him back for all those years. A long time had passed since I'd heard and felt those three magical words from him, and now, a new chapter of my life was beginning.

As I looked down at the chestnut brown eyes gazing back at me from my heels, words of joy tumbled loosely from my heart.

"I just got a puppy!"

CHAPTER TWO

FEAR

"You gain strength, courage, and confidence by every experience in which you really stop to look fear in the face."

~ Eleanor Roosevelt

Big, white eyeballs—that's what fear looks like to me. Eyeballs with the same shape and intensity of the full moon, decorated with tense, raised eyebrows and a wide, gaping mouth. It grips your belly like a greasy wrench on a clean pipe, and makes you feel all hot and shaky inside. I'm not sure I ever truly saw what fear looked like in an animal until I met Java. On our second day together, I gave her a new name. This bouncy dog was *certainly* not a Maddie, but I didn't *dare* name her Pogo.

Kaboing, Kaboing, Ka-no-thank-you!

It was our very first morning together—a cold, sleepy morning created from an interrupted sleep pattern of housebreaking rituals. Puppies get up to potty at two a.m. I had forgotten. I had also forgotten how stunningly beautiful the world is at that time of morning, and how exciting it is to see shooting stars when you're wrapped in a blanket waiting to praise the Potty Princess for her duties.

Grabbing my first cup of coffee for the day, I headed to my office to check my email and move some papers around. Clio and Veta barely moved their bodies from their throne position on the couch, but my new pup followed curiously behind my fuzzy, black slippers. Scooping her up into my lap, she curled her tightly-wound, little body into a ball and fell sound asleep. Heavy breathing changed to deep snores, as a trumpet fanfare blared loudly from her cold, wet nose. Looking down, I smiled at my new addition. She was a smart pup who I already admired. In less than twenty-four hours, this little being had easily figured out how to go to the door and bark to be let outside to potty. I was living with a genius canine. All that for only forty dollars!

Curled tightly in my lap, she looked like a fuzzy, brown and black woolly bear caterpillar resting peacefully on my legs.

Well, more like a giant caterpillar resting precariously. Taking a long, deep sip of my blacker-than-black coffee out of my bigger-than-big mug, I caught a quick glimpse of her smooth, dark, brindle coat out of the corner of my eye. In that moment, her true identity raced gracefully from my heart to my head.

Java.

Some people think that changing a dog's name is unfair. Others say it's a good thing—especially for shelter dogs. Me, I've always done what feels right. One look at this hound told me she had been hastily named in the car on the way to the shelter. So, with a quick brainstorm over a hot cup of coffee, Java and I clicked into a new life together.

Java lived up to her name. Filled with the robust energy only an espresso machine could expel, she was strong and dark with a tiny hint of sweetness. Bold, yet mellow. Sassy, yet distinguished. As the hours turned into days, Java's big, wide eyeballs were constantly reminding me of little, white surrender flags. Hesitance rested for moments, and sometimes minutes, on her sweet, little face as she explored her new world one fragile step at a time.

Where does fear come from?
Are we born with it or it is learned?

I think it's both. Java and I learned to experience fear together—and how to walk through it—but it wasn't long into our relationship before I realized that Java was afraid of almost everything. She was afraid to go outside alone, afraid of the cloth I used to wipe her muddy paws, afraid of the sound of wind, a leaf falling from the tree, my shadow, and her own. She was afraid of things on wheels, things that moved funny, things that sounded and smelled different. She was afraid of snow falling, snow shovels and snow blowers. Mittens, now that's another story. They were toys.

Soon, her eyeballs became accurate fear barometers, and I learned very quickly how to explain everything to her to help ease her anxiety. I mean *everything*. Keep in mind that I was a single woman with a lot of time on my hands. Java learned not only that it was a shovel we humans use to throw snow all over the place, but where I bought it, how much it cost, and why the neighbors had one, too. She learned that grass was underneath all of the snow and that it was okay to potty there as well. She learned because I explained in detail and encouraged her to try new things until I became exhausted. Then, I explained even more.

What transpired at a very young age was that Java started to check in with me when she became afraid. She'd notice something she deemed spookier than heads spinning backwards, and quickly gave me the 'whale eye.' You know, that sideways look where a slight hint of white shows and all of the uncertainty. I assured her uncertainty, rewarded her bravery, coaxed her gently, and loved her dearly and completely in every moment for being strong enough to show her fears to me. But I also wondered more and more *why* she acted so fearful and unsure of herself. Then, I started to look at my own fears.

Fear was something I hadn't spent a lot of time acknowledging earlier in life. I guess that's why my therapist told me years ago that I'm so resilient. There was no doubt I'd been fearful a lot in my life, but I always brushed it off somehow and forged ahead. And now, with the onset of a shy puppy, I felt different—almost justified to be who I was as well. I felt like I could acknowledge that I was a woman afraid of loving again for fear of getting hurt. I know I'm not the only being who's ever felt that way. I'm sure you've been in love before. Love can make the entire world go away—lifting every part of you, and allowing you to feel lighter and happier than you knew possible.

Yes, I'd been madly in love before. For almost my entire marriage I was head over heels in love. But as love changed to fear, I began to question whether it was healthy to live with so much fear. It felt painful, scary, and confusing to figure out what the best choice for me entailed, and it took me quite awhile to become clear. It's not easy to find clarity when you're scared. My fear came from knowing my husband and I were growing apart, and mainly just being afraid of what would happen *if* I had the courage to leave. I was afraid of the unknown.

After almost two years of inner work to find my clarity, I left my marriage in a loving manner. In order to remain true to myself, I needed to move. Somehow, I'd lost myself slowly yet steadily over the years.

How do you learn to love yourself again?
Patience. Time. Girlfriends.

If you've ever been afraid to make a choice you knew was right for yourself but might hurt someone else, you understand inner conflict. It's that sort of lumpy feeling in your belly that's all wiggly and icky, as if some sort of bridge collapsed between your head and your heart. Leaving my marriage felt that way. And after I left, I felt relieved but also frightened beyond belief.

How was I ever going to make it on my own?
What if this is as good as it gets?

Fear can tighten its hold sometimes and prevent you from making decisions in life. Although it was frightening, and I prayed like crazy that I'd be okay, I've never regretted my choice once. But, I was deathly afraid I'd never love again, and far worse, that I'd lose myself again in a relationship. To top it all off, I didn't have a clue who I was anymore.

What would I do with an entire free weekend?

How was I going to survive emotionally, financially, spiritually, physically and mentally?

I remember lying in bed my first night alone, asking the Universe to help me out. I surrendered to a place where I trusted that whatever was to be would be, and prayed for my physical needs first. I prayed for a small house to come my way with a yard that would make me feel like I was somewhere else. Then I prayed even harder to be able to pay my bills and live a simple, yet healthy life. I remember calling my ex-mother-in-law to ask if I was praying correctly. Like if it was okay to pray whether you were sitting quietly, lying in the bathtub, or scooping up dog poop. It is.

If you've ever lost yourself to love while you weren't paying attention, it can be pretty scary when you come out. You don't really know who you are, what sorts of things you like and don't like and, in my case, I was afraid to open my heart for fear of getting hurt again. My prayers were answered quickly. Feeling more connected to spirit than ever before, my trust meter was nearing full again. My house was exactly what I had asked for, and my financial needs were easily being met. There's a real gift in living alone. It allows you the time and space to process, rest, rejuvenate, and fall in love with yourself again. I sure did.

Was I ready to love someone else already?

Ready or not, there he was. Like magic, a new man appeared in my life about a month before my divorce was final. I was hesitant. I'd only been on my own for about four short months and didn't feel nearly ready to feel love for anyone else but myself. I never dreamed I could love again after a fourteen-year relationship, but the moment my eyes met his, something clicked. And now, here I was with this shy dog, a vulnerable woman in a blossoming world full of opportunities.

Cupid's arrow struck while I wasn't paying attention. It usually happens that way. Without any ulterior motives at the time, my boss (Ann) casually introduced me to a man who would teach me to overcome fear, and help me realize that we can have more than one love in our lives. A strong, firm handshake connected us briefly as I looked up to introduce myself. But when my eyes met his, a jolt of electricity created an image of bright red, animated hearts that swirled seductively around his head. My eyeballs, in response, quickly became little hot pink hearts that throbbed in and out like a cartoon. I'm not really sure if I actually let go of his hand and broke my gaze on my own or if I had to be surgically removed and hauled away.

With a roaring fire ignited inside of me that hadn't been kindled in years, I felt warm, free, and full of sexual energy just from a glance and a handshake. I also felt very juvenile. Within days of our first meeting, I took the leap toward love, and let all of my girlfriends assure me, reward me, coax me, and encourage me to go after this guy. Tall and lean with the most stunning steel-grey eyes I've ever seen, he touched my heart and soul gently, yet firmly. And in no time at all, I found myself being overly concerned about my appearance, and paying more attention to what came out of my mouth whenever I seized the opportunity to be near him. He was hot. When you're a juvenile, you come up with all sorts of code names for people so nobody *really* knows who you're talking about except your close girlfriends. That's exactly what I did. Red Hot was easily nicknamed after those irresistible, sweet, little cinnamon candies—the kind that rock your taste buds, but feel like they're gonna bust your teeth in half. I couldn't resist.

Red Hot taught me quickly how to overcome fear with love just by coming into my life, and allowing my heart to feel love again. He made me feel alive inside, like a schoolgirl who giggled and blushed when the cute boys walked by. He was a cute boy alright. Snug, blue jeans hugged a great rear, and dark brown boots told stories of where he'd been. A well-worn, brown, leather belt secured his button down, collared shirt from flailing all over the place, and showed off his trim waistline, too. His hands
were strong and well used, yet his lean, long fingers showed sensitivity, knowledge, and grace. Silvery, curly hair peeked out from behind a hat now and again, making me eager to run my fingers lazily through it. His voice was like a steady, sexy hum, and his broad, easy smile made my whole body sing with joy.

So how do you get to a man's heart?

Why, a puppy, of course!

Red Hot and Java met for the first time on Valentine's Day— just four short days after I picked her up from the shelter. On this specific day set aside for love, Ann, my school principal and boss, easily coerced me to head over to the building where Red Hot worked. Our mission? She and I would both drop off a bunch of homemade cookies for the guys at his office, making sure they were on a ceramic plate. Then, my task was to retrieve the crumb-ridden, ceramic, heirloom plate at the end of the day. *Mission accepted.*

Dropping the cookies off early in the day was simple. There's safety in numbers, and I didn't have to do anything other than stare, swoon, and control my drooling problem. But late in the afternoon, it was my turn to fly solo. When school let out for the day, I hustled home to check my hair, my smile, my teeth, and how great my butt looked in the pants I was wearing. Loading up all three dogs in my SUV, I mused at the thought of the pomp and circumstance I went through to retrieve an empty plate from a hot guy.

Women will find *any* excuse to get themselves near men they're attracted to. Me, I absolutely *had* to pick up an empty plate of crumbs, and figured I might as well see if he liked dogs at the same time. My heart pounded.

Baboom, Baboom, Baboom!

All of the workers seemed to be gone for the day when I arrived with steamed up windows, and a caravan of hounds. One, lonely car remained in the parking lot—one, golden, gem of a car that belonged to one red, hot man. As I walked slowly up the stairs to his office, my whole body felt weak.

Do I look alright?
Do I even remember what looking alright looks like?

I knew nothing about this guy, except how fabulous and alive I felt when I thought of him and saw him. That was enough to know for now, I guess. Looking up from my love trance on the stairway, Red Hot greeted me at the top with a stunning, bright smile and gentle eyes. He thanked me profusely for the cookies, then rested the empty cookie plate in my open hands.

"Um. Do you like puppies?" I stammered.

Stupid, stupid question! Who doesn't?

Why do our mouths open and garbage falls out sometimes? I didn't even say hello. I plopped out some sort of mindless babble!

"Sure," he answered generously.

Words flew out of my mouth like a roller coaster zooming down a steep hill, then flipping in a triple loop-di-loop.

"Well..., *(Baboom, Baboom, BABOOM!)* I just got a brand new puppy over the weekend. She's in the car. You wanna see her?"

"Okay," replied Red Hot, who seemed to be very short on words, yet quite concise.

Out to my truck we walked, while I carried the empty cookie plate and felt his strong, carnal energy near me. Then, time slowed to a similar place it had when I first laid eyes on Java a few days earlier—except now it was a place where I couldn't hear much except some sort of Barry White love song playing in my head. As my heart pumped love throughout my body, I caught a whiff of Red Hot's scent, and felt his steps get closer to mine. Somehow, I wanted to know more about him. As we neared my car, an image of Cupid caught the corner of my eye. She was waving a silver, glittery, wand.

"Wow! You have *three* dogs!" he said with exuberance.

He thinks I collect dogs. Maybe this was a bad idea. Why on earth did I have three dogs in my car to pick up a stupid cookie plate? Java, please help me. Work your magic, girl.

"Your pup is absolutely adorable. What's her name?" Red Hot inquired, as he tousled Java's head through the open window, then patted Veta and Clio on the chest.

He's interested! Breathe. Gather yourself.

"Her name is Java," I grinned proudly, then exhaled a huge sigh of relief. In that very moment, my heart knew it could love again.

What was this guy all about?
Could he possibly feel the same way about me?
Anything's possible!

Veta, Clio, and Java received more physical contact from Red Hot that day than I did, but it was the best Valentine's gift a single girl could've gotten. Hope.

I drove hurriedly back to school, cracked my windows, and locked my car doors. With very little composure, I sprinted to the door of the school, then ran up the stairs two at a time to return the prize cookie plate to Ann. I was out of breath yet more full of life than I had felt in years.

"Well?" she said with a coy smile, "How'd it go?"

"Oh, my God. He's *so* darn cute! It was great! And I introduced him to all three of my dogs, and he told me Java was absolutely adorable, and he smiled at me, and he looked right *at* me. I like him. I *really* like him!!"

Words fell clumsily from my mouth like odd-shaped tumbling blocks being whipped across the room by a small kid. Ann smiled and giggled at my happiness, and prided herself with how smart she'd been. She'd found a simple way to get me near a guy who rocked my single girl world.

"Well, I'll keep coming up with more silly reasons for you to see him so you two can get to know each other a little bit better. I'm sure I can forget things at his office a few times a week," said Ann as she chuckled with accomplishment.

There's an odd transformation that takes place when you walk through fear. It becomes excitement, or butterflies, as my dear friend Alana puts it. It seemed Java and I were on a mission together already—a mission to help each other learn, grow and change. Within four short days I had seen her face transform from fear to joy, and now she witnessed the same in me. For some reason, Java and I were matched up at the perfect time for both of us to grow.

When I look back, I'm not so sure I would have mustered up the courage to interact with Red Hot on that Valentine's Day if it hadn't been for the buffer my three dogs provided. They were security blankets disguised with fur coats, hot breath, and wiggly butts. Thank you, Veta, Clio, and Java. Eight days after my Red Hot Valentine's Day extravaganza, I met my very first soul mate at the Dane County courthouse in Madison, Wisconsin to declare our divorce final. Perched on uncomfortable, royal blue, plastic chairs in the lobby, we laughed and joked around like old times. When our number was called, we headed into a small room to declare our intention and sign a few papers.

Ten short minutes is all it took to erase a fourteen-year relationship. As we walked out of the courthouse together, we joked about wanting to throw a party to celebrate in some way. It felt out of sorts to simply walk away from someone I'd spent almost half my life with.

What do you say when it's all over?
Is there anything left to say?

We sat side-by-side in the front seat of my car and cried—not knowing what to do or say except to wish each other good luck and say goodbye. Taking the first leap on new legs can be really frightening, and also very exhilarating. Within the first week that Java and I spent together, we shared a wide array of strong emotions and intense events. I knew then that our hearts were strong and that we were meant to help each other make them even stronger.

With love on our side, and fear tucked neatly in our back pockets, Java and I made a pact to expand our worlds and tackle all that came our way with grace. So, the day after my marriage became legally dissolved, I held my breath, closed my eyes, reached deep into my well of courage, and asked Red Hot out for a cup of coffee.

CHAPTER THREE

ANGER

"I've learned to live with rage. In some ways, it's my rage that keeps me going. Without it, I would've been whipped long ago. With it, I got a lot more songs to sing."

~ Etta James

Inspiration comes in many forms. So does aggravation. And in my world with Java, I never knew when the lessons would present themselves. That's what I learned to love about her. She'd offer those little surprises that taught me quickly yet completely how to understand my own emotions better—to let go, laugh, and move on. Some days, she drove me absolutely nuts with her behavior. Other days, she made me laugh so hard I knew I couldn't live without her. Then, there were the days in between where she drove me nuts and made me laugh.

Fast-forward for a brief moment to four years later...
Today I returned to a different living room than I'd left a few hours earlier. Now able to be free in the house when I'm gone, Java met me at the door with all of her full body vigor, then quickly realized she neglected to destroy the evidence of her antics. Strewn about my entire living room, dining room, and kitchen was the most unique combination of items she has yet to put on exhibit. At first I was kind of steamed, but for only a slight moment. Then, I saw the lesson of humor in it all.

A dozen green and blue elastic bandages created a new floor covering at the doorway and beyond. At one time, each bandage was rolled up neatly into their tight little cylindrical form, and adorned with a cute little green and white turtle shaped diaper pin. Ribbons of colorful elastic twisted and turned, forming curvy, country roads across my carpet. Stepping over the sea of blue and green highways, I reached down to pick up the bits of the once intact plastic bag, which had once properly contained its contents. As my eyes left the first mess, I caught a glimpse of the second—an entire bag of Lemon-Mint Ricola® throat lozenges, each still neatly wrapped in their tiny yellow, green, and white wrappers, dotted my tan carpet like winged insects scavenging on the lawn. Java walked over to lick my face as a peace offering, while I turned my head to the left and let out a huge chuckle. Sometimes, when there's a really big mess, there's not much you can do but laugh. There was more. Covering the entire kitchen floor in an asymmetrical pattern of white rectangles, were my federal income taxes. Random claw marks and punctures in my 1099 and Schedule C showed marks of a Plott Hound warrior who was on the hunt while I was away.

Looking around my reorganized home, I must have looked at Java with disappointment, because she looked back at me with remorse. Sitting down on the floor amidst the mess, I took a deep breath, exhaled, then finally let a big smile come to my face. Java relaxed, wagged, and bounded through the house with joy. Think how much fun that must have been for her, and in one instant, my sour face spoiled the surprise she prepared for me.

Bad human.

Our emotions affect everything around us—positively or negatively. We can make a conscious decision to observe an emotion as it rises and let it go into a place of love, or not. We have a choice.

Anger has a rippling affect. It bubbles from somewhere underneath your toes and seeps itself out all over the place—affecting everything it touches. I never knew much about anger until about a year before my divorce. My therapist, Joan, (bless her fluffy yellow heart), was an amazing teacher who helped me understand what anger felt like, smelled like, sounded like, and looked like. For me, at that time, it was like a huge red-orange cave of molten lava I didn't dare enter. Anger sounded like the low, boomy echo of my father's voice, and it felt like something that would swallow you up and burn you. I remember vividly the day that Joan helped me walk into my molten cave of anger. I was very frightened and didn't want to go, but with visualization she assured me I'd be safe.

Hot. Melting. Unpredictable. What if I got sucked in forever?

An expanse of red, yellow, and orange filled my third eye as the heat of the cave of anger became clearer in my vision. I was afraid to go inside for fear of what I might find, but Joan respected my fears—taking it one, small step at a time. 'Chunking it down', it's called—a phrase I now use with my TTouch work with animals and my work with kids. With the door to the cave before me, I cried as I entered, and for the first time in my life I felt an amazing warmth inside my body as my anger became acknowledged and validated. What I realized quickly was that anger was nothing but a protector of the soft gooey insides. Kind of like milk chocolate covered caramels with pecans strategically placed.

From that day forward, I learned to say aloud "I'm angry." I learned how I use anger as a crutch to cover up my fear, and how I use fear to protect my sensitive heart. Rather than showing my soft side, I used to be a toughie. One time, in fourteen years, I told my ex-husband that I felt angry. I must have been angry more than once, but that explains how much I used to hold back. It all needed to rear its ugly head somewhere, somehow.

Anger teaches us about control or the inability to control. It's like the bubbly molten lava that has a heat, speed, and rhythm all its own but you can't do much about it—other than do your best to contain it before it blows completely out of control.

It took me awhile after my divorce to get through fear and find anger. I was angry—angry for the years I spent putting my energy into my marriage and losing myself in the process—angry with myself more than anything. Being angry with yourself really sucks. It's much easier to be angry with someone else.

Working through my emotions after my divorce was a process that didn't happen overnight but I sure wish it did. I spent loads of time lying on my rope hammock in the back yard, staring at the sky and letting my mind drift with the wind and clouds. Java learned how to jump *into* a rope hammock without having all four legs go through the holes. When the seasons changed, I spent even more time lying on my couch under a warm blanket and letting my mind flicker aimlessly like the candlelight that surrounded me. More time was spent writing in my journal, talking to family and friends, digging in the yard, creating art, being in nature, playing with my dogs, and continuing with my inner work through therapy. I had a lot of letting go to do and self-realization to find, and it took being on my own to figure out that the only thing I actually had any control over was myself. Balancing myself mentally, physically, emotionally, and spiritually became the next set of lessons the Universe offered me.

Then, there was Java. At only four months old, she was an innocent, little being who I wanted to help shape and mold to be the greatest dog on the planet—the kind who goes with you everywhere, fetches sticks, and doesn't need a leash. I must have been delirious thinking it was possible to have an easy dog, yet my first greyhound, Gabby, was like that so I knew it existed. I found myself getting angry at Java—wanting to control and force her to be different, or just settle down and grow up. I tugged on the other end of the leash to get her to walk right next to me, and I became angry that she pulled hard enough in the opposite direction that she made herself throw up.

Was she pulling on the leash and acting out because she was angry? Was I pulling on the leash and acting out because I was angry?

Most reactions from animals come from a place of fear, but at the time, I didn't know that. Anger is a human quality, but fear often looks like anger. What I started to notice from working with Java was that I would become angry when she reacted because I felt like she was a failure.

As time went on, a welcomed blessing occurred as my emotional intelligence increased. I began to own my anger and realized I was angry with myself for not knowing what I could do to help her besides pull back and yell "No!" I felt incompetent and sad when I got mad at her. It still makes me sad and a bit embarrassed sometimes, but it's all part of the process of learning, growing, and letting go. There's something transformational about anger if you can take a step away and become aware. It's an amazing teaching tool. Anger teaches you how you don't want to act and what you don't like about yourself. For years, my personal journal entries reflected perfectly my experiences surrounding my emotional growth.

Journal Entry
3/19/01 – Energy

I find myself becoming agitated when I give away too much of my own energy. I allow myself to blur my boundaries and let others get too close and invade my space. It makes me feel frustrated to try to control life, the dogs, and time. Sometimes, all I need is to allow myself to sit, be, let go, and be alone. I totally understand the desire to run, hide, and have life feel revitalized again when you return!

From trying to get Java to walk on a leash nicely or settle down, I realized how harsh I was. I yelled, stomped on the ground, pulled back on the leash, pulled up on the leash, and pulled half my hair out in the process. I felt terrible. I even swatted her rear more than once. I'd hold her tightly and restrain her body when she became feisty—thinking that would settle her down. All it did was make her panic and lose trust and respect in me. It also made me lose trust and respect in myself, and I didn't like feeling that way. It took time to forgive myself for misunderstanding Java. I tried everything I knew to change who and how anxiety-ridden and fearful she was—tossing penny-filled soda cans near her as she barked out the window; fitting her with every different choke collar and harness available to help her stop pulling; and exercising her every day just so she'd sleep and give me some solace. What I really needed to do was stop trying to control any outcomes. Outcomes come out all on their own if we let them.

Everything happens for a reason. Sometimes we aren't aware of what the actual reason *is* until a lot later, but it's always there if we're open to paying attention. At the time, I wasn't aware, but looking back, I now know. Java was anxious and fearful in order to learn for herself, and teach others about balance. In only a few short months she taught me about overcoming fear with love, to live in the moment, run until you can't run anymore, and jump until your legs give out. She taught me to love unconditionally, and that snow is a lovely commodity we're blessed to have in our lives. She made me aware of my own anger and that it was *me* who needed to change. She showed me that Plott Hound puppies can pee standing up on two legs if they try, and that there's nothing better than being held while you sleep in someone's arms. She showed me how puppy teeth can quickly pierce your nose, and that temper tantrums happen to young dogs right before they collapse for the night. All the while, my other two greyhounds, Clio and Veta, kept their watchful eyes on both of us. Veta continued to teach Java how to use her mouth, when to use her mouth, and where to use her mouth. However, eating fresh dog poop was not something I was grateful for, and I'm sure glad Java didn't listen too closely. Sometimes I wish Veta taught *me* how to use my mouth appropriately because there are times I could have used a big filter!

Clio quickly became the little old grandma who kept Java in line—beckoning me with a slight "Ahem" if there was something a bit askew; like a half chewed red, permanent marker on the carpet or a facial tissue that drifted swiftly to the floor. Clio was akin to Mother Teresa—unbelievably tolerant and never did anything out of line her entire life. I truly mean it. Both Veta and Clio did such a great job helping me raise Java, and all three of them loved each other like crazy. I loved them all like crazy, too.

As Java began to grow, our family dynamics began to shift. Veta and Clio started to use less energy to care for Java, so they were able to reserve energy for themselves. Everyone slept a lot at our house because we played so hard during the day. At about five months old, Java was making better choices about what to put in her mouth and what to spit out. She began having longer moments of stillness and wasn't quite as clingy or bouncy. There seemed to be a nice rhythm in our house for a couple of months, as I figured out how to care for my dogs and also care for myself. Finding balance isn't as easy as it seems. I'm one of those people who keeps repeating the same lessons over and over until I get them right. I'm still waiting to get stuff right, but if you've ever been in a place in your life where you wanted to punch the Universe in the nose for giving you the same lesson again, you understand. It's kind of like repeatedly bumping your head on a pipe in the basement ceiling so you can finally learn to duck or walk a different path—or learn to tolerate pain. There are always two sides to every coin and we can learn things the easy way or the hard way. As much as I had done a fabulous job of balancing my life, I was in for another reminder of how far there was to go.

Every couple of days, since Java was twelve weeks old, my three dogs and I spent time at a baseball diamond nearby to run free, blow off some extra energy, and smell the world. What an incredibly freeing experience it is to unleash your dogs, unleash yourself, and just run, play, laugh, and roll with them in the grass. On some occasions, Rebecca would show up with her three greyhounds (Bashie, Red Dog, Jenny), and her pretty-boy Saluki, Shadow. Our playtime multiplied with six, really fast dogs, and one Plott Hound puppy who idolized the fast ones. Java ran, ran, and ran some more when we went to the ballpark. Some days, she ran *away* from Bashie and Red Dog who often chased her, then knocked her over like a roly-poly bowling pin. There were a couple of days we had to haul the big boys away for a short time-out to help Java catch her breath.

What did we know?
Couldn't hurt anything, right?

In hindsight, Java seemed to be the one who was *always* being chased. She started to fight back by turning quickly and running different directions, sometimes chasing them, but she was too small and inexperienced for Bashie and Red Dog to take her seriously. Most of the time, Clio and Veta were body blocking the big males from running into Java.

It amazed me to watch the loving protection my other two dogs showed for Java. In hindsight, my ignorance was also amazing. I know now how hard the Universe was trying to hit me over the head with the lesson that Java wasn't truly enjoying herself. Running quickly away from *anything* with the whites of your eyes showing isn't a recipe for fun.

It wasn't always rough and tumble when we went to the park. There were far more days than not where Java was having an absolute ball, and there was complete harmony between all the dogs. A lot of days I would just take my three dogs, and they always ran well together. Veta and Java would engage in a game of chase, while Clio trotted the perimeter to pick up new scents.

Just watching my dogs run free together in a huge space was a sight to behold. When a greyhound kicks it into high gear, a huge rush of excitement fills my body. From low gear to high gear, their long, wiry body shifts into a blur that bends and contorts into a well-built racing machine. As the gear shifts into an even higher speed, their spine flexes up and down like a bendable straw, as their head forges strongly through the air before them. A thunder of feet rumbles below their muscular frame, each clinging hard to the earth for only one millisecond before flinging chunks of grass and dirt behind them with force. A greyhound can run at speeds reaching forty-five miles per hour. A Plott Hound puppy? About five.

When Java was six months old, and I was 407 months old, lightning felt like it struck both of us. It was a sunny, spring day and a bunch of greyhound guardians gathered at the fenced baseball diamond with our canine families. Eleven greyhounds and one Plott Hound sniffed, jumped, and ran free together as they'd done for months.

Watching from a distance, I stood peacefully in the grassy outfield with three multi-colored dog leashes draped loosely around my neck—laughing and telling stories with my friends as we watched the dogs romp, play, sniff, and chase one another. In a pack of greyhounds, Java always stood out as the slow one but definitely the smartest and most agile. Sidestepping any possible danger (or just to show off), she'd fake to the left, duck, fake again, run to the right, bound over the top of a dog, and keep on running.

Touchdown!

Java learned quickly how to maneuver her dense, athletic body in and amongst dogs that had been trained to run for a purpose. That purpose was to try to catch the fake bunny — the one who was kept just far enough in front of their skinny muzzles to make them run even harder.

Many of the greyhounds wore plastic, basket muzzles while they ran, which prevented them from sneaking in nips to cheat out the competitor. This was something they had gotten used to during their racetrack years. Of my dogs, Veta always wore a muzzle when she ran with other dogs besides mine. Clio and Java never did.

Breathing in the warm sun and cool air, I smiled deeply as the entire pack of hounds whizzed swiftly past us. The rumbling sound of thundering paws was felt beneath and heard above as chunks of grass and dirt flew backwards from their paws. Billowing clouds of terracotta dust quickly obscured the infield as a wide variety of legs, tails, bodies and heads created a graceful image of color, strength, beauty and mystery.

"Wow! Look at them go!" I squealed to Rebecca as eleven racing dogs created a blurry background for one spirit-filled Plott Hound puppy loping nearby.

Rebecca and I mused at the sight of Java's ears going up and down in an erratic pattern with her uneven gait. We watched the smile on her face widen as her big, pink tongue draped lazily out of her mouth and her chestnut eyes glistened softly with the joy of freedom. Java was having a blast. We all were. There are some things in life that are so stunning it's as if you could make a painting of one little snippet in time. Moments like watching a child bend over to discover ants crawling in a line on the sidewalk, or your first kiss, are etched in the memory of our hearts.

Like a movie slowing to one frame at a time, your lover glances over their shoulder, then smiles back before you part for the day. The look on Java's face when she runs is a painting yet to be created on canvas, but will forever hold a picture in my heart. It's times like that when you don't even need a camera because your body remembers. Yet sometimes, the memories aren't quite as beautiful.

Reeling inside from the joyous image of Java running past with a bright smile on her face, I felt the climate shift into darkness. On the far side of the infield in a small patch of lush, green grass, the elegance of motion came to a screeching halt. Like a flash of lightning, a piercingly loud, blood curdling sound hurtled its way to my ears and heart. When you know something is wrong, your body feels it.

Looking across the field, I glimpsed a frenzied pack of greyhounds in a large circle of motion and intensity. Java was nowhere to be seen. The blood in my veins rushed through my body with fear as maternal instincts easily took over. My stomach dropped three stories as I screamed toward the pack of dogs, then began to run in their direction with rage. The sound came again, but this time muffled and weaker. It was like the deep, guttural noise a pig might make if they were squealing in fear and then someone stomped on its belly.

Running across the field, my legs couldn't move fast enough as my eyes scanned feverishly for Java. My body knew the answer, yet my mind wanted to change how I felt. Intuition doesn't lie.

Where was she? Fear. Rage. Death. Hurry!

My heart raced with a strange combination of fear, rage, and compassion as I saw Clio and Veta frantically circling the pack to rescue Java. A quick glimpse into a brief opening in the action revealed my greatest fear.

There, lying helplessly in the grass on her back, was my sweet Java being pummeled by a pack of dogs almost three times her size. Images of black and white basket muzzles flashed into my line of vision, and I thanked the Universe for protecting Java's belly from the teeth-filled mouths that were snapping viciously at her. A few more weak grunts spilled out of Java's exhausted body as I ran closer with tears falling down my cheeks.

"GET AWAY!!!" I screamed in anger, as I forcefully whipped my three leashes at the pack.

The dogs scattered quickly, leaving Java a bit dazed to shake off what had happened. My jaw was hanging open in disbelief, and my heart was absolutely crushed. Java and I connected for a brief glance, then she was off and running again. Me, I was ready to go home. The other dog owners were close behind, also wondering what happened, as we all leashed our dogs and headed out the gate in silence.

What made the dogs turn on her so suddenly? Was she hurt?

Anger? Yes, I was angry—angry at myself for allowing it to happen, and angry at the other dogs and humans for allowing it to happen. Red, hot, molten lava. I was angry like a mother ready to kill anyone who harms her baby. Good thing I have better self-control than that. I felt terrible for Java, and I was also worried whether or not she was truly okay.

Rebecca called later the same night to see how Java was acting and to find out whether she was hurt or not. I told her she looked fine and was crashed out on the big, flowery ottoman like she always had done after a run. It didn't appear to have caused any damage.

But things changed not long after Java was attacked. It's like a definitive line was drawn with a jumbo, red crayon — showing us how things were now going to be different and more challenging.

More challenging?

With Veta and Clio both aging and becoming less involved in Java's upbringing, Java started to exhibit bully behavior. She began to push me out of her way at the doors, to push for her dinner, and be pushy, pushy, pushy. She began to react aggressively when she saw other dogs, and exhibited a lot of anxiety when visitors came over by jumping close to six feet in the air when they arrived and doing wind sprints until they left. Very few people were willing to visit my home, and of those who did visit, only true dog lovers were willing to stay for any length of time. We had a definite problem and it showed. We were *all* out of balance. Clio started to become more aloof and spent more time alone, while Veta became moodier, snippier and a lot more work. I started reading books about dog behavior and learned to feed all three dogs separately, and focus more attention on Java's issues — to teach her how to sit calmly and ask permission instead of demanding. I know a few people that could use that sort of focus and attention.

Immersed in a world where my daylight hours were spent teaching hundreds of children how to paint, draw and be nice to one another, my evening hours were spent trying to find my own balance among three unbalanced dogs. Those of you who have multiple dogs (or children) in your home can relate. At first, the changes at home seemed pretty subtle. In time, as I began to piece it all together, the day at the park changed our lives. I became more protective of Java and more concerned about her behavior. My own anxiety increased, and I found myself worrying, wondering and making judgments about my own life and others. I felt responsible for Java—for why she was so jumpy, barky, snarly, wiggly, hyper, pushy, sproingy and doingy, yet she was the most loving animal I ever met.

I'm kind of jumpy, barky, wiggly, hyper, pushy, sproingy, doingy and loving!

Our walks became so miserable that I wasn't physically or emotionally capable of controlling her. Java wasn't physically or emotionally capable of controlling herself either. She was pulling harder, and so was I.

So, instead of trying to control Java, I let go and decided to get control over my own self by seeking advice from a colleague at school. Mara taught special education, and worked mainly with kids with emotional and behavioral issues—the kind of kids who throw chairs and swear. The ones I love the most.

She and I were lucky enough to score classrooms next to each other and were often found locked in a quick bear hug each morning—giggling, and telling stories before the bell rang. I trusted and respected her, and we shared our stories as a daily ritual.

Walking into work with my coat barely off, I whined to Mara, "I can't handle this anymore. Java almost ripped my shoulder out of its socket last night on the bike trail. I *hate* feeling frustrated."

Mara smiled, then replied lovingly, "Why are you pushing her so hard? Walks aren't fun for either of you right now, and Java needs to go at a speed she's capable of in order to be successful. So do you."

"It's funny," I replied, "in my heart I know what's right, but I keep feeling like I'm supposed to be doing what society says is best. You know, like you're supposed to walk your dog three times a day, and it's supposed to be enjoyable. I feel like every time Java and I are connected by a leash, we're miserable."

She went on to tell me about a particular student we both knew who could only handle being in math class for twenty minutes before books, pencils, chairs, and profanities flew across the room. If she kept him in the room for fifteen minutes, he felt relaxed and good about himself. If she pushed him to twenty-five, he'd backslide and wouldn't want to go to math the next day—feeling like a failure.

After talking with Mara, I followed her advice, listened to my own intuition, and stopped taking Java on long walks for six months. After dealing with my own feelings of guilt about what society said I was supposed to do with a dog (walk them daily, play ball, go to the park etc.), I let go to the fact that the back yard of my house was a fenced half-acre. Java got plenty of mental, physical and emotional exercise and still played with Veta, Clio and Rebecca's dog, Shadow. Since Java seldom stopped moving at all, she got plenty of exercise just being who she was, so I began to focus on showing Java what relaxed and comfortable *truly* felt like.

Java and I spent a lot of time sharing our lives together, watching a variety of songbirds flock to the feeder, or taking naps side-by-side on the couch. By slowing down and backing off, we were able to pay more attention to the world around us, each other, and ourselves.

At the same time I was teaching her, she was teaching me. I started to feel more balanced and centered from sitting and enjoying the stillness each moment provided. Resting the body balances the mind and spirit. I learned that from Java.

Around this time, my anger kind of dissolved into a place of letting go. While learning to sit and "be," I came to a euphoric place of inner calm—a feeling I hadn't visited much since I was a child nor thought about much. Through working with Java, we were both showing signs of being out of balance and then finding our balance.

Like a pendulum swinging back and forth, Java and I went from one extreme to the other until we rested peacefully at a halt in the center. There's a reason that clocks stop once in awhile. The pendulum needs to catch its breath. I knew there was hope for both Java and I, but I could sense an imbalance with Clio and Veta, and I was concerned. Clio was spending more time alone, and Veta seemed like she was poorly wired. My house was filled with swinging pendulums.

At the beginning of that summer, Clio's health began to fail. She had been diagnosed with histiocytosis about a year prior—a cancer that fills the bloodstream and overtakes the organs slowly, sometimes painfully, and always fatal if left untreated. Clio's first tumor was undiagnosed and resulted in amputating half of her helicopter-wagging tail about five years before. Her second tumor came about three years later—a year before Java bounded into our lives.

When Clio's second tumor came I was still married, and we found a tiny growth on her chest a month after she lost her best friend and greyhound companion, Gabby. I often wondered if the cancer was related to Clio's grief when Gabby died because our bodies hold our emotions if we don't let them go. Clio seemed to hold on to everything. Because of Clio, I learned to let go of my own emotions, and receive openly from others.

Clio and I had a history together and shared a sacred bond and a lot of secrets. After I left my marriage and moved out on my own with Clio, I asked her if she could stick around until my feet were on the ground. She was a rock in my life, and I wasn't ready to let her go. Clio was ten years old so I made a conscious choice to forgo chemotherapy and radiation. I wanted her to have a quality life, although it may be shortened, so I let her be and loved her more each day.

If you've ever made a difficult choice for another living being, you understand how heart wrenching it can be. You might wonder if it's the right choice, and also question what gives you the right to even *make* the choice for another being at all. In many ways, I think animals are saints for putting up with humans. Clio was definitely a saint. I wanted the best for her, and I felt a sense of freedom and calm when I decided against the cancer treatment that was offered.

Following your intuition is about trusting yourself, and I was finally learning to do just that. Clio and I had a lot of quiet, intimate times together. She wasn't a dog who ever played or roughhoused, but rather asked permission to lay in the sun all day in peace. As she aged, she rarely got up unless it was necessary—like eating, pottying, quietly reprimanding Java, or to kindly greet someone new at the door. She was one of those gentle spirits who taught me how to give and receive love, and the importance of giving it deliberately.

As Clio and I laid on the floor together during a daily love session, her spindly front legs wrapped gracefully around my neck while her hot, stinky breath blew straight into my face. Whispering softly how much I loved her, Clio gazed lovingly back to me with her dark brown eyes which were becoming more clouded and discolored with age. She stretched and sighed as I stroked the folds of her thin, black ears slowly, then ran my hands gently around her delicate head and narrow muzzle, noticing how grey she was.

Continuing on, I rested my hand on the shiny, black fur on her neck, then stroked down to her strong, right shoulder — continuing to share my secrets to her in a quiet whisper. Another stretch and a long moan, Clio peeked for a moment then closed her eyes in complete relaxation.

Resting my hand firmly on her warm, broad chest, I felt her heart beat slow yet strong beneath my palm. With very little hair on her underside, the skin on her chest felt loose and soft, and the warmth of her chest made me snuggle in even closer. As I moved my hand slowly down the right side of Clio's deep chest, my heart sank. Underneath my fingers, I felt a small, round growth about the size of a small pea.

We had been through a lot together since the last tumor surfaced three years before and I wondered if her body was reminding her that it was okay to cross over. I laid on the floor with Clio for what seemed like an eternity and cried. I promised her I would do whatever I thought was best and told her that I truly *was* going to be okay.

As I dialed the phone to call the vet who'd cared for my greyhounds over the years, my mind was already made up. I would do whatever it took to make her feel comfortable and live out the rest of her life with the regal pride this queen deserved.

"There are a couple of options. We can do surgery and remove it, or you can let it run its course. At her age we'd have to do an ultrasound to make sure her heart can handle the surgery and that the cancer isn't housed in her hear," my vet explained stoically.

Cancer in her heart? This dog was the founder of unconditional love. It must be elsewhere.

In my own heart, I knew I needed to do whatever I could for her. If you've ever been in a similar place with an animal, you understand. I had learned how anger had controlled me in the past, and I didn't want it to control me anymore. Anger had wasted a lot of my energy, and I wanted to be done with it—done stomping my feet to try to make things the way *I* wanted them to be.

Life doesn't work well when you try to force it. What I soon came to realize was that there's extreme freedom in letting go of anger. I learned that what's left underneath is sometimes just a soft, fuzzy, blanket of wonder and anticipation.

Two weeks after I was told of Clio's cancer, I let go of wanting to control the outcome, and took her to the clinic for an ultrasound. And after five long months of wondering, worrying, and stomping my feet, I finally anticipated my first date with Red Hot.

CHAPTER FOUR

PATIENCE

"Rushing into action, you fail.

Trying to grasp things, you lose them.

Therefore, the Master takes action

by letting things take their course."

~ *Lao Tzu*

I sat quietly on the sunny, warm sidewalk outside of the vet's office and waited. Rivers of salty tears streamed gently down my face, scattering little, wet, dot patterns on my faded, pink t-shirt. My mind drifted to a time two years earlier when my husband and I were faced with the decision whether or not to euthanize our other greyhound, Gabby. And now, I was a single woman, faced with making a serious decision by myself. I felt horribly alone.

Was I making the right choice?

Sometimes when you're alone you feel really alone especially if you're *new* to being alone, which I was. In a time like this, when I needed to make a big decision, I felt more alone than ever before. Small teardrop marks across my chest were sweet, soggy reminders of letting go. I found myself daydreaming while the hot, July sun warmed my body, and images of peace and love filled my heart with softness. With eyes closed, I inhaled warm, summer air deeply into my lungs and smiled. My mind emptied completely like a huge sheet of black construction paper, and my body felt as calm as gentle waves lapping up on the shore. Time floated away to a place of nothingness, and somehow I managed to find myself in a beautiful place of stillness during a time of potential crisis.

Imagine the times you've been faced with a crisis in your life. How did you choose to handle it? Did the crisis handle *you* or were you able to set the crisis aside and tell it you'd be back in a little while? It's not an easy task to find stillness amidst crisis, but when you are able to do so, it energizes you for anything that might come next. Patience creates space.

My sunny place of stillness was quickly jostled by the jingling sound of the clinic door opening. Turning my head to see what creature was making that noise, my veterinarian walked toward me as I held my breath in anticipation. My body tightened with worry.

Was she okay?
Did she die?

Joining me on the sidewalk, my vet looked into my tear-filled eyes and softened her face. Young tears began to take shape in her eyes.

"Clio's okay right now but when we did the ultrasound we found that her cancer is like a spider web that fills her entire body. I don't think her heart will make it through surgery but it's your choice. We can try if you want to."

Single teardrops became a rushing river washing over my already tear-stained cheeks. Lowering my head in silence, a whirlwind of emotions filled my mind and heart. Words struggled to form themselves on my quivering lips.

What was the best for Clio?
How would I feel if she died in surgery?

My vet sat patiently and waited for what seemed like an eternity for me to respond. Swallowing slowly, I caught my breath, and looked over with red, puffy eyes. It's times like that where a deep sigh tells an entire story all its own.

"I just want to take her home," I squeezed out amidst sobs.

"I don't blame you at all. I'll go get her," my vet responded kindly, with big tears in *her* eyes now, and a gentle hug for me.

Gathering myself off the sidewalk, I walked inside the clinic and began writing a $500 check for Clio's ultrasound. What

I was really doing was paying for peace of mind—knowing I'd made the right decision. I wasn't willing to risk her life in order to remove one cosmetically ugly tumor when her entire body was filled with cancer. At this point in Clio's life, she was losing her eyesight, had only part of a tail remaining, three canines left among many other poor teeth, and a five-inch scar on the side of her body. I wasn't the least bit concerned about having a pretty dog. Money and beauty don't matter when there's a life at stake.

Looking up from my checkbook, my whole body smiled as I spotted Clio bounding happily from the back room—wagging her half of tail stiffly yet vigorously from side to side. The happy look in her eyes and her bouncy body language reaffirmed my decision. I knew in my heart we were going home to let Clio live out the rest of her life. More pressing than that, I needed to get ready for my first date in almost fifteen years.

Clio stretched out and moaned with joy in the back of my SUV, sunning herself on a grey and white comforter that cushioned her bony, old body. While she was resting gracefully on a cloud of love, I was brimming with anxiety about being with a man. Java and Veta greeted Clio with numerous wags and kisses, and the energy was filled with excitement, relief and a whole bunch of peace and calm.

I felt unbelievably relieved to be bringing Clio home in her original form—without a shaved chest, bloody stitches and a plastic cone around her neck. Java bounded playfully toward Clio, then licked her muzzle as if she had never felt so happy before in her entire life. Clio of course obliged by standing patiently to receive, while Veta stood nearby rolling her eyes at the doggie love affair.

Then there was the pomp and circumstance of preparing for the human love affair. I'm not so sure getting ready for your first date after a divorce classifies as being put in a chapter on patience, however. I was ready in about eight minutes and spent the next two hours looking out the window, looking at myself in the mirror, and moving unimportant things around in the house just to fill the time.

My stomach brimmed with butterflies as my heart pounded like a bass drum in anticipation. As the clock ticked closer and closer to my first date in what I'd dubbed *The Year of Love*, my mind raced with wonder.

What if he tried to kiss me?
What if he didn't?
Did I even remember how to kiss?

Red Hot showed up at my doorstep at 5:00 on the button. I was taken aback by how surprisingly normal and unbelievably handsome he looked in civilian clothes. I'd only seen him in work clothes for the past six months and I even thought *that* was sexy.

Here he stood before me, wearing a pair of tan shorts, brown leather sandals, a tan and black plaid shirt, and no hat hair. He looked *great* and I made sure I did, too—with just enough skin showing to make *him* wonder and *me* feel a bit naughty.

"Wow, you're prompt!" I said stupidly.

Red Hot smiled a bashful smile back toward me as I opened the screen door to let him inside. A sea of exuberant hound dogs flooded my entire living room.

Boy, I hope this guy can swim!

Java headed up the pack, bouncing up and down before my date like a caffeine driven alien on a brand new pogo stick. She appeared to be completely ungrounded, and I'm not so sure I appeared much different. Directly behind both Java and I, keeping all four feet on the ground and wagging stoically, were Veta and Clio—fully composed. It's hard to impress a new guy when you're competing with three dogs.

Red Hot and I walked around my house nervously, looking at this and that, and making idle conversation that filled the space with nothingness. My stomach rumbled vehemently, like an old Harley on a wide-open road, as thoughts of intimacy filled my mind. I felt like I was either going collapse, throw up, or else run at top speed in the opposite direction!

You call this butterflies?

Veta and Clio were quickly bored with the bland home tour but Java kept right at our heels, finally settling to a place where she could sniff, focus and actually process who had walked through the door. If I were a dog, I would have bounced up and down like a caffeine driven pogo stick when Red Hot showed up at the door, too.

Who could blame a girl?

I found myself feeling unbelievably shy and self-conscious, and who knows what kind of nonsense came out of my mouth. I didn't have a clue what to do with a man in my house, let alone a man who made me feel this kind of nervous excitement. Java followed us outside and quickly darted for her favorite toy—a red, plastic bucket from the hardware store down the street. Grabbing the rim of the pail in her strong jaw, she flipped the bucket completely over her head, then entertained us as she ran around blindly at top speed.

Thoughts charged through my head like a freight train engine while Red Hot appeared cool and calm. I wondered what he was thinking, wondered what I was feeling, and was grateful for Java's silly antics to break the awkward silence. We laughed at Java's antics for awhile as she raced around the pine trees in a figure eight, plowing down any plants who dared to peek up and say hello. Red Hot watched in amazement as huge clumps of dirt, grass and hostas catapulted from Java's feet and flew like misfired arrows across the yard. It was definitely time to leave.

"How about we head to dinner?" I suggested nervously, as Ms. Red Plastic Bucket Head came flying to a screeching halt at our feet.

"Okay," replied Red Hot in a very concise manner as he followed me toward the screen door.

Still not long on words, is he?

Heading inside the house, I grabbed a treat for Java on my way through the kitchen, while Red Hot waited calmly in the dining room. Java's big, pink tongue drooped loosely from a wide smile, and her face showed a fabulous combination of exhaustion, joy and mischief.

"In your bed, girl," I said as I opened the door to her crate, then tossed the biscuit inside.

Java ran full force from the kitchen, and slid forcefully from the front to the back of her crate on her blue, fleece blanket like a well-trained stunt dog. Saying goodbye to Veta and Clio, I gave them each a treat, told them we were going to dinner, and reminded them to please take care of the house while I was gone.

Exhale.

With all three dogs in their places, Red Hot and I walked out to my car together in silence. As he stretched the seat belt across his lap, I noticed him peer over his left shoulder and pause for a moment. Glancing in the rearview mirror, I realized that lying peacefully in the back of my car was the grey and white blanket I used to ease Clio's ride home from the vet earlier in the day.

Red Hot and I engaged in a bit deeper conversation as we drove to the restaurant—both of us wondering more about the other it appeared. I felt much more relaxed, and it seemed that he did, too. We talked and laughed easily throughout dinner—sharing stories, learning more about each other, and remarking about the lovely pink and orange summer sunset.

After dinner, we drove back toward my house, and I had every good intention of making it to my friend Carrie's birthday party later in the night. However, it appeared that the Universe had a different plan. Red Hot looked over at me with a bit of apprehension as we neared the end of our dinner plans, then asked nervously, yet firmly,

"Hey, you wanna go to the park and hang out for awhile?"

YESSSSS!!!!!! YESSSSS!!!!!! Ahem. Compose yourself.

"Okay," I replied. This time *I* was short on words.

After a quick stop at home to let my dogs out to potty, we headed to a nearby park to extend our time together, and see what possibilities lie before us. My heart skipped beats like little dragonflies flying up in the air to perform stunts, then skimming across the top of the water with grace. Red Hot grabbed the grey and white blanket from the back of my

SUV, and we walked slowly down a wide, grassy trail toward a lopsided park bench. Sitting down, I exhaled at the natural beauty around me and the calmness within me. Red Hot scooted next to me, then rested his strong hand on my leg just long enough for me to sense his warm heart. We sat for a few minutes in silence, but this time the silence was really gorgeous. Completely alone with Red Hot—surrounded only by sounds of insects, birds, and small critters—I was in single girl heaven.

As the sun continued to set on the horizon, we headed up the trail to a small clearing in the woods, and set my blanket on the cool earth below us. Time completely stopped as we spent the entire night sharing stories under the stars, amidst the bats, coyotes, and mosquitoes. A magical moment it was—the kind that rests itself gently in your heart, like a feather drifting slowly to a halt.

Yes, he kissed me—more than once. I remembered how to kiss back, too. Filled with tenderness and wonder, we were two people learning more about themselves and each other under the strong, white light of a full moon. I hope you've done something this freeing in your lifetime. If not yet, then some day.

As the morning sun began to peek out of the horizon, I wrapped myself in the grey and white blanket as Red Hot and I retraced our steps through the woods and back to my car. Opening the car door, I chuckled at the rectangular gift that was neatly wrapped in purple and orange tissue paper—waiting patiently to be delivered. I had completely missed my friend Carrie's birthday party, but I *did* have the intention of going. Girlfriends understand unplanned moments of lust.

We drove in silence and exhaustion back to my house, as Red Hot dozed off and on in the passenger seat. I wasn't really sure what to do with a sleeping man in my car, nor what to do with him once the car stopped in front of my house. I was concerned that he might fall asleep at the wheel, yet I didn't know what was the right thing to do.

"You wanna come in and get a little sleep before you head home?" I asked in hesitation.

"Okay," Red Hot replied in his signature, simple manner, then unbuckled his seat belt and followed me up the walkway to my front porch.

Java, Veta and Clio were *very* grateful when I opened the front door and said hello.

Where in the hell were you?
Is this what men do to you—make you irresponsible?

I could feel my dogs screaming at me. I guess I deserved it. I certainly *acted* irresponsible for the mere sake of having a good time with a guy. Java was incapable of settling after being kenneled for almost nine hours and I needed her to be different. So, out to the back yard all three dogs went while Red Hot and I laid around, dozed off and on and talked.

Between loud crashing sounds of terracotta pots hitting the cement, Java periodically popped her chunky, brown head up into the window to peek at what was going on. Every fifteen minutes or so I'd whip another bone outside to keep her preoccupied. I laughed nervously at the destruction occurring outside while trying to find solace with a man inside. After a short nap and some breakfast, Red Hot took off down the dusty trail, and headed home. My first date in fifteen years had me reeling with the possibility that my heart was going to be okay. Actually, it was obvious that is was going to be better than okay. As I let the dogs in from outside, I thanked each one of them profusely for putting up with my single girl antics.

A week later, I flew to Arizona for a weeklong vacation with my best friend, Ellen. Our goal was to hike in, and hopefully out, of the Grand Canyon. If you've ever done that hike there's absolutely nothing I need to say. If you haven't done it, be sure you're in good shape before you go and make your reservations for any time other than July. That's why I love Ellen. Just a few months before, I phoned her and asked if she wanted to share my birthday with me in the Grand Canyon. Of course she did! Surprisingly, there was only one room available at Phantom Ranch at the *very* bottom of the Canyon for our hike in, and only one at the South Rim at the *very* top for the night of our hike out.

It was meant to be.
Let's go!

Off we went—two dumb girls and a backpack full of squashed bagels, warm water and trail mix. We started out all happy and chipper at five a.m., heading down the South Kaibab Trail with ease. We smiled at how simple it was. There were paths! Then the mules started to pass us by in droves as we laughed about the similarities to the Brady Bunch Grand Canyon episode.

There we were; singing songs, laughing, and looking at rocks, rocks, and more rocks, while I belted out one of my favorite Etta James tunes. I felt like a rock star as my voice echoed freely throughout the Canyon, "Out of the raaaaiiiin, under the shellllter. I've been so loooonng, where the sun don't shine. Standing at the crossroads.....I can see long ways, I feel love again....It took your sweet love, to pull me ouuuuut of the Canyonnnn."

Ellen laughed hysterically, then chimed in. After an hour of listening to the same song over and over, she kindly asked me to shut up.

Then, the sun came up. Like a joke heckling from behind the Canyon, it reared its ugly head and laughed a menacing laugh at us. Our bodies felt the exhaustion as the heat seared our skin, and sweat evaporated immediately into nothingness. My backpack, once filled with gallons of water, was getting lighter and lighter yet neither one of us felt like we needed to relieve ourselves. The blisters came next. Our toes pounded down into the toes of our boots with each step creating more pain in our bodies. As we stopped to rest and put duct tape over the worn skin on our feet, a perky troop of Boy Scouts passed us by with whistles of joy.

Little creeps!

We gagged down warm water and trail mix at each resting point, then choked down the rest of our pride as we continued down the trail. At 5'10" and with two bad knees, I was in trouble. Halfway down the steep trail I was already wearing my second knee brace and popping pain relievers like tropical fruit jelly beans. My scrawny knees felt like they were being poked and prodded with little ice picks, as each step became an excruciating effort that was punctuated by the pain of what felt like bones crunching on bones in my tall, skinny legs.

Patience is something you learn sometimes when you put yourself in a difficult situation. It's one of those virtues that has many faces before you actually get to the patience part. There's the part where you're so pissed off you want to scream and quit, and the part where you're in tears and giving up. It's the giving up part that gets you to the patience part, however. Think of the times in your life when you've been on a schedule and something beyond your control happens—forcing you to learn about patience or else suffer. Usually, when a cop pulls you over, you learn about patience. Standing in line or rush hour traffic can teach a lot about patience—or impatience.

I stopped talking to Ellen for the last hour and a half of the hike down because nothing nice was coming out of my mouth, and I wanted to remain friends. My head became filled with thoughts of having my half-eaten body found by a bunch of archaeologists three hundred years later, and I could hear voices in my head that were laughing at me.

Boy, that's really too bad.
They should have brought more water.

As the heat continued to drain my energy, the pain in my feet, knees and hips turned my focus inward. When you experience that kind of immense exhaustion and pain, it's almost as if it's so bad you just forget about it. My attention turned completely to a place inside of me that was deeper than I had found before in my life. I always knew I had strong willpower, but the last mile or so of the hike into the Grand Canyon pushed me further inward than I had experienced thus far. However, I still wondered how on earth we were going to hike out the next morning!

Journal Entry

7/31/01 - The Super Duper Grand Canyon

It's so beautiful how aware this hike has made me – the shape of each rock I pass, the sound of nothing, the texture of the earth crunching underneath my boots, the world waking up slowly as lizards and snakes scurry through the brush and birds' songs echo in the canyon. We passed very

61

few people along the trail and one ranger seemed amused by our laughing and my singing. I serenaded Ellen (until she was ready to knock my block off) with Etta James' Out of the Rain. The color of the Canyon changed the lower we got inside and the blues and greens started to replace the sand and dark red.

On the hike down, railroad ties became steps, and rocks became obstacles. The pain in my knees prevented me from enjoying the beauty. My left leg was completely numb from my hip down to my foot and my left foot felt like it belonged to someone else. My body poured out what seemed like gallons of sweat when we reached the bottom, and my heart pounded with exhaustion. I felt like I was turning inside out. Hot. Sweat. Heat. Pain.

The temperature at the bottom of the Grand Canyon was 112°F, and when we started our hike at the South Rim it was 54°F. My body shot quickly into cramping stage, and my mind drifted to the hunger pangs in my belly. Ellen and I perched ourselves next to one another on a huge rock for awhile and sat in complete silence—trying as hard as we could to notice the immense beauty at the bottom of the Grand Canyon. It truly *is* stunning, but it takes getting *out* to appreciate it. Getting out was coming tomorrow, hopefully. We waded in Bright Angel Creek in more silence, and I took a sip from the bottom of the Canyon while Ellen snapped a memorable photo.

Walking with hunched over bodies and limping limbs, we hobbled to an old, wooden bench in a clearing nearby while scents of Ben-Gay® wafted through our nostrils. Bracing our pain-filled bodies for a change from vertical to horizontal, Ellen and I laid on our backs on the bench, head to head, and watched the birds fly above.

Breezes washed over our tired bodies as our minds focused in on more looming questions. There can either be a lot of distance created from silence, none, or somewhere in between. In that moment, Ellen and I were closer than we'd ever been—the place where words aren't needed because you already know what the other person is thinking.

Turning her head toward mine, Ellen whispered softly in my ear, "We're gonna get out, you know."

That's all I needed to hear—faith.

I ate more that night than I knew my body could hold, while Ellen passed on the fabulous vegetarian buffet and decided to eat warm bagels from our backpack. I was concerned that she wasn't eating enough to restore her energy for the hike out the next day, but we still weren't talking much to one another. We were both in a fairly introspective space—doing what we needed to do to prepare ourselves mentally, physically, spiritually and emotionally for the next day.

With a somewhat good night's rest, we woke up at four a.m. to prepare for our hike. Filled with extra strength pain reliever, Ben-Gay®, and a protein bar, I felt ready to rock and roll. Then, I stood up. Gritting my teeth in excruciating pain, I sat back down to assess my options, and tighten my knee braces.

What was I going to do? I could call a helicopter to get me out, or gather up the inner strength I didn't know I had and get out on my own.

Strapping my dark green backpack around my shoulders, Ellen and I headed toward the trail head with the determination of two warrior women. We didn't speak for most of the hike out; not because we were angry or so immersed in the beauty of the moment, but because we couldn't. Every ounce of energy we could muster, needed to go into our own personal journey at this point. Somehow, we both needed to find the deepest part of ourselves—our will—in order to continue on and remain focused. I was surprised to find that hiking out was much easier than hiking in, and that the crunching sound that came from my knees on the way down was not quite as apparent.

Hey, this will be a piece of cake? Liar.

White, soft sand scattered lazily beneath my boots, intermingling with the red, clay dust from the hike down. Ellen stopped briefly to pick up a discarded, plastic, water bottle, while I spotted a brown bat in a cave in the rocks.

Who litters in the Grand Canyon? Someone!

We stopped every half an hour to let our bodies and minds rest along the way and welcomed a bath in the streams to cool off. On one of our short breaks, we stopped long enough to witness a feisty, grey squirrel trying to steal our bag of trail mix from atop Ellen's backpack that was lying on the ground nearby. Like suburban warrior goddesses, we defended our rations by waving our arms, and screaming profanities at the bold squirrel. He didn't *dare* take what crappy food remained! It's amazing how much we cherished that trail mix at the time, and how much we take for granted now. When you have very little, very little is a lot.

As the hike continued, I had an epiphany. We are all so caught up in the destination that we barely take time to stop and notice how glorious the journey is. Halfway through the hike out I was forced to lift one leg up at a time—to feel the gritty sand slip underneath each step, to feel the energy of each plant as I passed by, and become one with all that encompassed each moment. When you're in that kind of a meditative state, you can breathe in and feel a tree in your lungs, and exhale your breath and feel it fill up the Canyon.

For me, the Grand Canyon hike was an elaborate feast for my senses, a great spiritual awakening, and the greatest test of my own self-will. I was blessed with the sound and sight of California condors grasping a safe place in the rocks to feast on a kill, the simple sound of the wind rushing past a leaf and nothing else, and the sight of the long winding trail behind us and ahead of us. We *did* make it out—in ten hours.

Patience *is* the Grand Canyon. There's nowhere to go but down and up. There are no clocks anywhere, so you're up against your own body, mind and spirit. You can hurry along and pass it all by just to get it over with, or you can succumb to what is, slow down, and enjoy each step along the way. That's exactly what I applied to Java the moment I got home from that trip. I began to take the time to slow down and enjoy each step along the way instead of hurrying her to get to a place *I* thought was best.

When summer ended and fall began, Java and I enrolled in our second obedience class at Dog's Best Friend—a well-known training establishment founded by Patricia McConnell, (*The Other End of the Leash*; Ballantine Books, New York). Soon into the class, I saw teeth. Java's teeth. Java and I started the six-week class in a circle with the other people and dogs, but we were quickly surrounded by our own small circle of white patio chairs.

This offered Java both a visual and physical barrier from the other dogs, and although it was very successful, I still felt like a huge failure with a freak-show for a dog. The trainers gave Java and I great support and suggestions during the class, but I was embarrassed for the dog I had. My own lack of self-confidence started to show and made it difficult for Java and I to communicate clearly.

Safety became an issue so Java couldn't work off-leash during class. She lunged at other dogs while I gripped the leash. Although some parts of the class were challenging, there were many moments where I was very proud of both of us. Java was eager to please, and willing to do anything for treats, so obedience came quickly. It made my heart soar to watch how hard she tried to stay focused with me while she was greatly concerned about the other dogs near her.

We stayed in class for the entire six weeks, but by the time it ended, I knew we had our work cut out for us. Java felt my disappointment when we left each night for our long drive back home because the look on my face was obvious, and the silence in the car was telling. I was mostly disappointed in myself for putting her in a place of danger when she was attacked by the pack of greyhounds, and I was embarrassed that I didn't have more knowledge. Little did I know, knowledge was in our future.

It's no fun to be disappointed in yourself. It usually means you have some forgiving to do. Forgiving yourself can certainly be a challenge, and for me, forgiving myself has always been a challenge. I've made a lot of mistakes in my life and I continue to learn from them, get back up, and keep on fighting. With Java, I definitely made mistakes and needed to come to a place of acceptance and forgiveness. I wasn't there yet, but Java was. Animals accept and forgive a lot quicker than humans do.

Java and I worked really hard together to practice what we learned in class. We gave our secret handshake then crossed our fingers and paws in hopes that things would change. Be careful what star you wish upon.

Journal Entry
10/22/01 - Stars

Went out with the dogs last night, and the sky was crystal clear...filled with tiny, gleaming stars and cool, crisp, fall air. I can feel the energy of the stars—the Universe outside—within me. This morning I saw a shooting star, wishing upon it for love as it soared from west to east in a short path. The first one I saw this summer went from south to north, and I wished on it for love then, too. Does that mean that all directions have been balanced with love? Where do the stars go during the day? Do they just get sucked back up into the sky?

As the leaves began to fall at a rapid rate, my second dog, Veta, began to change even more. At nine years old, Veta came to me from Wisconsin Greyhound Pets of America three months before Java plopped into our lives. She and Clio hit it off right away with their gentle spirits, and I was happy for Clio to have another dog around again.

Veta's racing and vet history was a mystery because her records were lost by her previous owners, so there were a lot of pieces missing to this furry puzzle. The only information I had was that she was a divorce dog, which meant that neither party wanted her. That's a tough break for an eight-year-old dog who raced off the first four years of her life at the track.

A brindle and white greyhound with fur as soft as a bunny, Veta was an odd combination between a clown, a nervous wreck and a devil. On many days, I'd come home from work to witness dozens of plastic bags forming an Olympic-size skating rink in the living room, and not a hole in any of them. The next day, maybe an array of sponges, napkins and pot holders were the toys of choice. She was adept at opening cupboards and drawers, trash diving, mischief and causing a great deal of work for me. She also made me laugh quite a bit, and practice my patience. I learned quickly that in order for the garbage to be left alone, I needed to move it. And if I didn't want her to place plastic bags all over my house while I was gone, I could put boring stuff in the cupboards and drawers, or get drawer locks. Sometimes it takes awhile for wisdom to take hold.

It's much more common to want to change the dog rather than change our own habits. When a dog pulls on a leash, fix the dog, right? When a dog barks at everything passing by, address the dog's barking, don't you think? Well, what about your end of the deal? It's not always the dog's fault that they behave the way they do. Sorry to blow a hole in your theory, but it took me a bit of time to realize I was part of the issue–usually more than half of it.

Creative problem-solving means finding more than one way to solve a problem and finding a way that maybe forces you think outside of the box a bit. We have a choice about whether to try to solve a problem or not, but we don't always make one. Sometimes, not making a choice at all is what keeps us stuck in unhappiness.

Veta taught me a lot about the power of having a choice. My choice was to find a better home for her—one that could provide a better life for her than I could—or continue to live in imbalance. Rehoming a dog can be one of the most loving choices an animal caretaker can make, and also one of the most difficult choices. Your mind and heart don't always agree, and it takes a long time to decide what's right. Sometimes you never really know what's right.

Veta was a challenge. She was one of those dogs you don't completely trust because you don't know how she's going to react on any given day, in any given situation. Soon, I began to question her health when she started to snap at Clio, Java, and I. My first thought was thyroid because ex-racing greyhounds are notorious for having thyroid issues that can often be the cause of aggressive behavior. With a barrage of tests and more money, we ruled out thyroid.

Then there were her severe intestinal issues, which were a common occurrence for Veta, and a nuisance for the rest of us. I cooked bland food for her for months, and my vet put her on antibiotics to rule out infection. Veta would be 'normal' for a few days, but nothing seemed to work with her long-term, and I was getting frustrated, becoming financially strapped, and feeling more tension building.

Test after test showed nothing, and then I thought about my house. I lived with three dogs, and Veta was the only one of them who seemed horribly unhappy. She experienced frequent intestinal upsets, dug enormous holes in the yard, was a poop eater, and guarded her food and toys. I'm not one to make a hasty decision, so we lived in this chaos for over a year. Something specific usually happens to force a greater change to take place.

It was a cold day in December, and the sound of chickadees chirping outside my bedroom window roused me from my sleep. Wrapping myself in anything warm from nearby, I headed to the living room to let Java out of her crate to go potty. Then, I turned my head to follow the rancid scent that was wafting from the dining room. A huge, brown puddle awaited action in the middle of the floor as Java leaped over it with ease, then continued happily to the back door to go outside. Veta chased after Java, running straight through the brown puddle, then followed her outside to eat something wrong. That was the final straw for me, and I dialed the phone in frustration.

"Helllllpppp! I have parent/teacher conferences tonight and Veta's crapping all over the house," I told Rebecca through tears of frustration.

"Bring her over," she replied, without hesitation.

With a long school day ahead of me I dropped Veta off at Rebecca's house and never picked her up. Inside, I knew I needed to find a better home for her, yet I felt like a huge failure. In all honesty, I felt guilty for getting rid of a dog. Rebecca assured me I wasn't the only person on the planet who'd rehomed their dog, and that most people don't try as hard as I did, cry as much as I did, and make heartfelt decisions about what's best for the animal. Okay, I felt a little bit better.

Journal Entry
11/30/01 - Connections

It's incredible how we feel the immediate connection (or don't) between beings. Everyone or everything we come in contact with serves a purpose—to align our personality with our soul. When I talked with the dogs on Monday about Veta leaving, I had three very different reactions. Veta knew what was going on and seemed sad but understanding. I don't really know if she and I connected or not, but it felt like we did. I talked with Clio next, telling her I was thinking of finding Veta a better place to live. She looked me straight in the eyes and burped in my face! Gross!

Clio and I have this quiet connection that usually runs deep. We both know. We've both lived with each other for 8-1/2 years. With her, it's just calm. Then Java, who comes running to my side at the mere onset of tears. She and I had a really deep connection from Day One. Our souls clicked. So, I tell her what's up with Veta and I'm standing in the bathroom. *I ask her what she thinks of Veta going away and she lowers her head, looks toward Veta in the living room, then back to me with a sad look on her face. Then, I tell her that maybe she and Clio will get closer. With that, Java walks into the office, kisses Clio, comes back by the bathroom door, lays down, and looks right at me!*

The energy in my house was very different when I came home from work that day. With only Clio and Java remaining, there was a feeling of sage and sinner. Veta had definitely bridged the gap between my cancer-ridden Clio and my adrenaline-ridden Java. Now, with only those two dogs left in the house, their gap seemed to lessen in many ways. Clio seemed older and more fragile, and Java seemed more balanced and grown up. Java was moving from her juvenile position in the batter's box, and stepping up to the grown-up plate.

I walked outside with my two hounds and watched the bright, yellow sun merge with a kaleidoscope of colors before it went to sleep for the night. The crisp December air made me shiver inside and filled my lungs with a brisk freshness. Pondering the deeper things in life, I peered over to look at Java and Clio and explained to them what happened—that I'd truly sent Veta away to find her a better home. Dogs understand a lot more than we give them credit for. Me, I was sad. I cried until my tears ran out, then I turned toward Java in amazement. Looking more closely at her, I noticed her normally slender abdomen was swollen to the size of a football. It certainly hadn't been that size earlier in the day. After a bit of investigation in the back yard, I discovered she had devoured an entire loaf of rye bread left outside for the birds. Gas.

If you've ever wondered what happens when you gently squeeze a football-shaped Plott Hound, it's kind of evil, and a bit funny and entertaining. Java tooted like a queen-size squeaker toy, and I found myself amused by how much air her body could hold and release, as I watched the entire shape of her body shift back to normal. It reminded me so much of the first day I got her, and how skinny she became after she relieved herself. Bless Java's heart for making me laugh so freely in those moments of difficulty.

As the moon came up to say hello, the three of us headed inside for bed. Grabbing a dog biscuit on my way through the kitchen, I reminded Java to go in her crate, then I kissed Clio good night. Like clockwork, all of us filed into our respective sleeping quarters as we'd done together since the beginning. The moonlight cast a strong light into my bedroom as shadows of the night danced across the room. With the warmth of three heavy comforters holding me happily in place, I thought about all of the changes that had transpired in such a short time.

Suddenly, a loud howl pierced its way from the living room to my ear drums. Java. It was a sound I'd never heard from her before so I hurried to investigate. Wiggling and whining in her crate, she seemed strangely agitated. It was our first night without Veta so I wondered if she missed her, or if she didn't. Somewhere deep inside me, I knew the answer to my own question. As soon as the thought hit my brain, Java sat quietly at the door of her crate, wagged her tail, then looked at me with her head cocked slightly to the left.

"Okay, you. Here's the rules," I explained as I unlatched the door to freedom. "We *sleep* at night and you need to be a big girl and stay out of trouble."

Java looked back at me, shook on the deal, and hopped into Veta's old resting place—the big, yellow, puffy chair in the living room. Heading back to my warm bed, I smiled at my peaceful Plott Hound perched high atop her throne, then passed through the office to ask Clio to keep a watchful eye, just in case. Java slept soundly that night and every night after that. We'd made a deal. With Veta gone and Clio starting to fail, Java knew she needed to move up a notch on the maturity scale, so she did it perfectly and with pride.

Veta went to her final home soon thereafter. A grateful, 62-year-old woman who lived alone with no other pets took her in, and her issues resolved themselves. I felt glad she could now live the calm life she deserved but in some ways I still felt a little badly that I couldn't fix it all myself. Sometimes we have to gently close the door and let go of our ego.

When one door closes, another opens. Veta left and Red Hot showed up again. Six months had passed since our romance in the park. Why so long between dates? I suppose the Universe gave me the time I needed to figure out what I was ready for, and to decide what was the healthiest. We were both given time, but there was some sort of magnet that pulled us toward one another every now and again. Although we both felt something special, it wasn't a relationship that felt healthy to either one of us.

Did I really want to have one date every six months with someone I thought about almost every day?
Nope.

My head knew the logical thing to do, but my heart wanted to change my mind. I once read a fortune in a fortune cookie that read "Nature, time and patience are the three best physicians." I had learned how to wait patiently for the answers to find themselves among the questions, yet now I found myself wavering between my head and my heart to find the truth. I didn't want to wait any longer for any more answers, so it was time to consult my crystal ball. Whenever I found myself in this sort of predicament, I relied on the wisdom of my parents. My Dad always said, "If it feels good, do it." Then my Mom would remind me, "When in doubt, don't."

For a long time, I didn't understand what those two contradictory phrases meant, and I wondered how I was ever going to make a healthy decision with that sort of advice. As I grew older, it was easy to choose between the two. When my body felt uneasy, I didn't proceed. When my mind wavered back and forth, I didn't proceed.

What I took from my parent's wisdom was that if there's indecision in your head, your heart, or both, it's best to wait until there's clarity and calm. Patience taught me all I needed to know, because the answers always came if I waited long enough. The anxiety in my belly told me that I needed to make a decision about what was healthiest with regard to my sporadic relationship with Red Hot.

Wavering ever so slightly between my head and my heart, I drifted peacefully to a place of inner knowing, and gently closed the door to the Red Hot chapter in my life.

Click.

CHAPTER FIVE

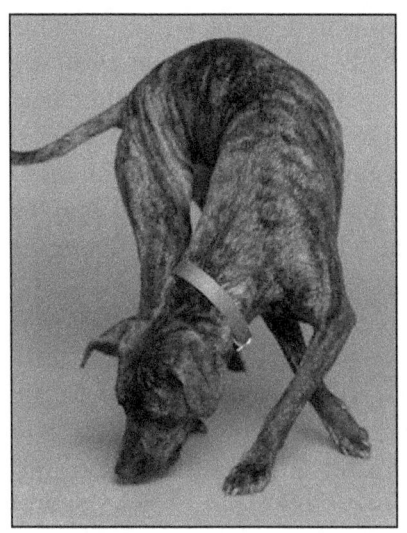

AWARENESS

"Everything has its wonders,

even darkness and silence,

and I learn, whatever state I may be in,

therein to be content."

~ Helen Keller

Enthusiasm prevailed during my first full winter with Java. I learned to love huge drifts of white, fluffy snow again. As a child growing up in Wisconsin, I spent winters skiing, sledding, and dodging snowballs and face washes from my older sister, but somehow along the way I had forgotten how to be a kid. Java helped me to remember. At the end of most school days, she and I were often found chasing each other in the back yard—laughing, tossing snowballs and playing soccer in a snowdrift, while Clio perfected her lounging skills from inside under the covers.

Tossing huge, poorly packed snowballs in the air, Java would accept my challenge—catching face-fulls of fluffy, white snow that disguised her entire being. With only two brown eyes peeking out from a blanket of white, she'd shift her eyes to one side and her body into a play bow. She was on fire and ready to get me back.

With her rear toward the sky, and a mischievous wag of her tail, Java would bound straight toward me like a flash of lightning and steal a soft, fleece mitten swiftly from my warm hand. A game of chase would begin and we'd often end up rolling together in the snow in piles of joy until my soggy, freezing cold mitten was surrendered. Then, she'd steal the other one, and we'd start all over again.

Who's teaching who?

When we take time to play, we make time to become aware. With the hustle and bustle of the work day world knocking at our door, we sometimes forget how many precious moments surround us. Java taught me quickly how to walk away from the stress of work so I could learn to play like a kid again. Having a young dog is a great excuse to remember how to laugh, hide, and roll on the floor. Do you remember?

Think of the times when you are totally immersed in something you love to do. I mean something that makes the entire world melt into a puddle—a place where clocks don't matter. Maybe it's cooking, dancing or planting flowers. Or maybe you get lost in the moment when you play basketball or fix things around the house. Whatever it is for you, it's vital that you find it, nurture it and continue to harvest it. Deep play keeps us young at heart and teaches us how to find the spirit in everyday living. It also keeps us healthy. Java and I laugh and play every day whether I want to or not.

We had an abundance of playful spirit at our house that winter and I found myself spending more and more time lying still and allowing thoughts to drift in and out of my consciousness. I prayed frequently and felt like I was on the edge of finding out new things about myself, and about life. At the same time, I wondered what else was out there. Some people have a name for that—spiritual seeker.

Many people are brought up with organized religion. I was brought up watching the Green Bay Packers professional football team on Sundays. Living with a Jewish father and a Lutheran mother, my sister and I often found ourselves eating French toast, playing outside and having our Dad read us the comics instead of attending a church or a synagogue. Both of my parents had a strong faith growing up, and both of them vowed they'd never force their kids to choose, but as I grew older, I wondered what I had missed. I had questions about faith.

Did I have any faith?
How do you get some?

There was a time, about two years before I left my ex-husband, where I became more aware of the power of the Universe. Surrender does that. Sometimes when your world seems upside down, all you can do is let go and allow change to take place. Hopefully, you'll land softly on your feet instead of bouncing off your head. During that time, I became more aware of feeling connected to spirit when I was outside among the trees, rocks, dirt and wind, and that if animals could be a part of the picture, all the better. It was in nature where I felt my true spirit come alive. I've tried churches, synagogues and even praying in the shower, but what I learned over the years was that my faith was very strong, yet I didn't fit into a specific mold. I guess I've never fit into a mold. Thanks, Etta.

It was partially through the music of Etta James, that I first found my true faith and strength. Growing up a musician, I easily found strength in music, but Etta's music was different. It reached far into the depths of my soul and made me shake my groove thing like a hot, Latin maraca player on the beach. Etta found her way into my life years ago when a neighbor brought a cassette tape over to my house for a dinner party. When Etta started to sing, my whole body lit up from head to toe. That's faith. You can find it in the smallest and largest of places, and it doesn't have to be inside of a building on Sunday. Etta's music made all of the hairs on my body stand up and pay attention, and I wanted to know more about her.

After work the next day, I bought a compact disc of Etta James and took it to work the following day. While playing Etta's signature song *At Last* during a third-grade art class, a little African-American girl asked me who was singing on the radio. Sitting down next to her, I smiled. With a background as a musician, I was often found teaching kids about different styles of music, and introducing them to a variety of musicians. Music had always been an important part of my life, and even though I was an art teacher, I wanted my students to be exposed to different styles of music. Even my third graders knew who Ella Fitzgerald was. However, they honestly thought her name was Elephant Gerald.

"This is Etta James," I told the little girl as she listened intently, "I heard her for the first time a few nights ago. She makes me feel happy. Do you like her?"

"Oh, yes!" the little girl replied quickly, then continued, "Is she dead?"

I had a propensity for introducing my students to dead musicians. In my opinion, most of the great ones are gone, so the question made me smile, chuckle and wonder myself.

"You know what? I don't know if she's alive or not," I told her truthfully, as I walked over to the CD player and picked up the black and white insert from the disc.

Inside was the title of a book that was to change my life. Etta James was very much alive, still performing and had recently published her biography, *Rage to Survive* (De Capo Press, New York). At the time I read that book, I needed the rage to survive. It's amazing to me how much kids can teach us.

What evolved from a simple interaction between an eight-year-old kid and a thirty-four-year-old woman that day was my incredible passion for Etta James. My collection of Etta James CDs multiplied dramatically, and I set my intention clearly—to meet this fabulous woman in person some day and shake her hand. I never underestimate the power of Miss Etta James.

When we're walking the path of a spiritual seeker, we never know where or when our teachers and guides will present themselves. What we do learn, however, is to pay attention.

Awareness is key, because if you're not watching, you might miss a fabulous opportunity for growth. For me, Etta James was a fabulous opportunity, and she made a huge spiritual impact on my life. I also knew I couldn't only belong to the church of Etta, so over the years I continued to seek out other things that reached the depth of my soul. I looked for the kind of stuff that makes the skin on your body vibrate with electricity. Java does that to me.

Sometimes in our lives we're lucky enough to have an animal who feels more special to us than any other—the one who shares with you a deep, soul connection you can feel but you can't see. Dogs like Java are the ones who show up at the perfect time and place to remind us about humility. They teach us lessons we need to learn, learn from us the lessons we offer to teach, and share with us an incredible spiritual relationship.

My Mom always said, "You'll have one dog in your life who's more special than any of the others."

My Mom was right.

It takes patience to become aware of the magic that surrounds you. For me, awareness came with the stillness I learned to manifest within myself. I noticed small things I hadn't paid much attention to before—like the one blonde eyelash Java had on her left eyelid amidst the row of black ones. I noticed the extreme stiffness in her entire body, even when we went for short walks just around the block. It appeared as if she had big, steel rods running through her back legs and that her skin was stretched taut, like a high-pitched snare drum head, over her dense, muscular body. Her face showed concern, and she seldom turned her head or sniffed the ground, but rather stared forward in hopes that we were done soon. I became aware that Java seldom wagged her tail while outdoors, and that it was almost always held stiff, high, and curled from the tension in her hindquarters. I noticed the dryness in her mouth, how tightly she held her lips against her teeth, and how much white showed in her eyes. I became more and more aware of my surroundings, myself, and my animals by learning to sit still and carefully observe the world around me.

I also became aware of the tension in my own body, and how much I held my breath, clenched my jaw or slumped my shoulders with poor posture. All it takes to become aware is slowing down and paying attention. Easier said than done.

Java and I spent a good part of the winter balancing outside playtime with snuggling under the covers together. We searched for answers to life's difficult questions, while Clio snoozed peacefully in her bed in the office. She'd already figured out most of the answers anyway. I felt more centered than ever before and had come to a place of happiness that I hadn't experienced in the past. My breath was longer and fuller, and I seemed to stand up straighter and smile more. Java seemed to be able to lie still for longer periods of time, and she was able to move slowly from one point to another. We both became more aware of our bodies, and realized we could actually be in control of how and when we moved them instead of flailing about. Java and I were guiding each other to learn about awareness. Me, I wanted to become even more aware.

When the student is ready, the teacher arrives. Flipping casually through the pages of a local magazine one day, an advertisement caught my eye. The ad was promoting a shamanic practitioner who did journeys for soul retrieval and power animal retrieval—whatever *that* was. What kept coming to me as I looked at the ad was nature, rocks, animals, and drumming. With very little hesitation, I phoned the woman in the ad and set up a session for the following week—not actually knowing why I was going to see her, but trusting the knowing I felt deep in my belly. Over time, I had learned how my body felt when I was content, upset or feeling change on the horizon. Somehow, this shamanic work seemed familiar.

Journal Entry
3/31/02 - Resurrection

It's Easter morning and today I see Ana, the shamanic practitioner. I looked up the meaning of my name on the Internet and it means 'Resurrection.' I wonder if I can live up to that! Who knows what today will bring but there's excitement and energy in the air. It's the end of Lent, the start of April, the end of my spring break and the start of a new chapter and new beginning. I'm going to see Ana with an open mind and heart—just curious and excited. I'm in a good place right now. Yesterday I got an email that Etta James is playing in Madison on my birthday! How crazy is that? Thank you for such wonderful gifts. Thank you!

As I navigated my way through downtown Madison, I wondered what kind of experience lay before me, and smiled at the memories that were behind me. With the methodical click of my right turn signal sending me into a trance, I turned down a familiar side street for a drive past the house my ex-husband and I had bought when we were newlyweds. Loads of fond memories made their way gracefully from my head to my heart as I traveled four more blocks to Ana's house. I was in a really good place.

Knocking gently on the door, it opened to reveal a beautiful, woman smiling before me. Dressed casually in loose, dark brown cotton pants and a matching shirt, her earthy apparel made me feel immediately at ease. A colorful array of tiny, stone, animal carvings danced playfully around her neck, and a long, dark braid swung like a pendulum down her back. She was *definitely* a teacher for me.

"Come in. I'm Ana," she said warmly, with her wide, loving smile welcoming me into her home.

"Thank you. I'm Sage," I smiled back, as I felt the kindness in her handshake.

We went upstairs to a small room containing a wide variety of what appeared to be sacred objects. Feathers, candles, drums, rattles, and sage filled the room, as Ana thoroughly explained the process of shamanic journeying to me.

"What brought you here today?" she asked gently, as a gorgeous tortoise shell cat snuck into the room and rubbed against me.

"I don't know. I just knew I needed to see you," I responded, stroking the content feline who had now taken up a semi-permanent place on my lap.

"Most people come for healing, but you're different. I think you just need direction so you can learn and guide others," Ana smiled at me as she asked her lump of a cat to please wait outside during our sacred ceremony.

Lying flat on my back in the sage filled room, Ana proceeded to call in her animal and spirit guides from the east, south, west, north, above, below and within. Powerful songs, whistles, and gentle shakes of the seed-filled rattle sent me quickly into a dreamlike state as the heartbeat of the drum filled my mind with colorful images. Ana guided me safely on my first of what would become many shamanic journeys, as I dove deeply into the moist earth of the lower world to find and retrieve my main power animal. We then worked together to help heal old spiritual and emotional trauma from a car accident I'd experienced two years before. There was drumming, nature, rocks, animals and so much more, and I knew I'd found a way to seek guidance for myself and others.

For the first time in my life, I felt like a spiritual warrior princess—ready to face whatever challenges might come my way.

CHAPTER SIX

UNDERSTANDING

"Living is easy with eyes closed, misunderstanding all you see."

~ John Lennon

Life seems scary and wrong sometimes. The moment my mother gave birth to me, I was hung upside down, swatted on the rear end, took a huge gasp of air, screamed at the top of my new lungs, and was forced to open my eyes. It's hard not to hold a grudge about being born in a traditional hospital in the sixties; big smiles two inches from your face, cold, pain, tears, bright lights, blood, sweat, and loud noises. Years later, I've learned to open my eyes and see. There's a big difference.

We can live with our eyes open and still live an enjoyable life, but it takes living with your *heart* open to understand the depth of life. When Red Hot and I said goodbye to one another, my heart finally knew how to understand. Understanding is about unconditional love—requiring you to let go and surrender to what is. It allows us the choice whether to accept or suffer. I wanted to be done suffering in my personal life, my professional life, and in my work with Java. We were ready to make a go for it.

I'm sure you've heard people say, "Be careful what you wish for." There's a lot of truth in that. When you make a wish, you need to be very clear—otherwise, the Universe gets kind of confused. It's not always easy to be specific about your wishes, but when you're aware of the power of the world around you, it's worth the extra effort to try.

Almost a year earlier, a thought went from my head straight to my heart then plopped out of my mouth.

I want to find a way to make money petting animals.

Even more so than that, I wanted to find a way to work with *both* kids and animals together. In my heart, I knew the time had come to start letting go of a future that had me teaching full-time in the public schools. I had become bored as a school teacher, which is a recipe for disaster. When teachers are bored, they're doing a disservice to kids. Winning awards, getting loads of recognition from colleagues, and appearing on television and in the newspaper for my work as a teacher was incredible, but the daily grind wasn't doing it for me. As an art instructor I worked closely with 500 kids during the course of each week. I knew every kid's name and something unique about each of them—like who got their hair cut, what color their eyes were, what tooth recently fell out, and what made them tick. It became exhausting not to be able to connect more deeply with the kids because I really wanted to in some way. I loved every single kid for some reason or another, and sometimes I just loved them for no reason at all. I felt like an art factory shuffling them in and out of my room twenty-five at a time, and I wanted more for myself and for them.

Soon I was researching various animal-related careers that would allow me to make money. Bless my mother for supporting my choices since I was a kid because this one sounded like I was going to put a handwritten sign in my front yard that read "I'll pet your dog for 50¢." I looked into animal massage first as a career and then looked for schools nearby that could train me. But when I spoke with the director of the Veterinary Board in Wisconsin, I was informed that animal massage was not then a licensed or certified career, and that I may have difficulties finding work if I wasn't associated with a veterinary clinic. The sign in the front yard started to seem like a good idea. When I make up my mind about something, I start to pay a little closer attention to the signs around me. When your intention is clear and concise, really cool things start to happen.

It was a Monday evening in March, when my girlfriend Wynne called to ask if I wanted to come to Chicago for the weekend. While I talked with her on the phone and made plans for a short road trip, I doodled on a tiny slip of purple paper on the dining room table. Alongside my doodles was the name of a guy who was an animal massage therapist—a name I had scribbled down because I thought I'd check it out anyway. After securing our plans, I hung up with Wynne and fondled the paper in my hand.

Was this what I wanted to do?
I want to make money petting animals!

I stopped listening to the voices in my head long enough to listen to my heart. Phoning the man on the purple slip of paper, he explained a little about animal massage training as a career, then told me it would be best to talk in person. I was somewhat eager that he was so interested in explaining his career to me, and I agreed that I'd learn the most from seeing the work being done. But how?

"I'll be at the Pet Expo in Chicago this weekend," he said nonchalantly as my jaw dropped rapidly.

"Umm...that's crazy. I just hung up with a friend and planned a trip to Chicago this weekend. I guess I'll see you on Saturday."

About this same time a green, hardcover book fell off my shelf. The cover showed a blondish woman with a Siberian Husky—both engaging in a beautiful embrace of concentration, relaxation and love. A fellow animal lover and colleague lent this specific book to me almost two years earlier, and I was embarrassed because I still hadn't read it, or returned it. Leaning over, I picked up this book that voluntarily levitated itself onto my carpet and read the title: *The Tellington TTouch®: A Breakthrough Technique to Train and Care for Your Favorite Animal – by Linda Tellington-Jones and Sybil Taylor* (Penguin Books).

Looking back, I now realize how hard the Universe was working at unveiling a path for me to follow. I could have made my life a lot simpler by being more aware of some strong signs, but I wasn't ready yet, so I put the book back on the shelf.

A friend stayed with Java and Clio for the weekend while I sought out girl time and animal massage. When I arrived in Chicago, I had a few hours to spare, so I headed straight for the Pet Expo. Walking through rows and rows of essential oils, fancy dog collars, and newfangled inventions for pets, I felt excitement in my belly. Being among dog people felt like the perfect combination of challenging and comfortable, and at the same time I had no clue what most of this stuff was. What I did know was that it was the type of stuff that made me lose track of time.

Deep Play.

I found myself immersed in amazement at an entire convention center filled with resources for animals, and I felt a special kinship with the people I spoke with. In some ways, I felt like an outsider coming into a familiar place. Having a challenging dog like Java, I also felt like an insider who shared a special kinship, but was looking for more knowledge to help us both.

Heading to the upstairs level at the convention center, I had every intention of spending a large chunk of time with the animal massage therapist I'd spoken with on the phone earlier in the week. But the moment I turned the corner and spotted him, something didn't feel quite right. I've learned to listen to my intuition now, but back then I still questioned it once in a while. Walking over to his booth, I introduced myself, listened to what he had to say, thanked him, then walked away. The strange feeling in my belly hadn't

89

completely subsided, so I finally paid attention to what my body was telling me and what my Dad had taught me. It didn't feel right, so don't do it. As soon as I walked away from the animal massage booth, I ran directly into a booth about telepathic animal communication—almost knocking over the small, round table with a pastel-colored tablecloth. Catching myself from a calamity, I noticed a small clipboard of names resting on the table alongside a sign indicating private animal communication consultations.

Maybe she could find out what's inside Java's head? Maybe I could become an animal communicator!

Picking up the black, ball point pen from the table, I prepared to sign up for a fifteen-minute animal communication session later in the afternoon. As I looked more closely at the sheet, it was completely full for the entire weekend. I was disappointed. In that moment, it felt like a waste of time for me to be at the Pet Expo. Even though I wanted to find a lucrative way to pet animals for a living, it seemed the Universe was plotting different plans for me.

Then, I turned around. Like angels surrounded by metallic gold rays of light and singing the Hallelujah Chorus, I saw it. Tellington TTouch®. Like a shy cougar checking out the surroundings before it pounces, I walked carefully over to the booth with a slight bit of hesitation and a huge bundle of curiosity. Immediately, my eyes caught the same green book with the woman and Siberian Husky on the cover—the one that took a nosedive off my bookshelf earlier in the week. Was it divine intervention? Coincidence? Synchronicity?

"Hi. I'm curious about this work. Can you tell me more?" I eagerly questioned the two people in the TTouch booth.

Without my sentence even being finished, the man and woman were busy explaining how they were going to have a training starting in spring of 2003 in Chicago, and I needed to sign up, and here's a pen, and….. I wasn't even sure what Tellington TTouch® actually entailed but I knew it had *something* to do with petting animals—petting them so *they* felt better, not just me. Their enthusiasm showed me right away how incredible this work must be, so I signed up on the mailing list and felt hopeful.

At the end of a fun weekend in Chicago, I was eager to get home, hug my hounds and find out more about this animal work called Tellington TTouch®. The TTouch web site (www.TTouch.com) showed there was a five-day training being held in Minneapolis only six weeks away. My eyes raced through the web site with the excitement of a child with an orange balloon, finding out that TTouch was so much more than just petting animals. Tellington TTouch®, it said, is a gentle method of working with animals, based on respect, understanding, trust and love rather than fear and force. It is a method that helps to reduce stress, engages the brain and helps to balance animals (and humans) mentally, physically and emotionally. When I read the part about helping an animal balance emotionally, my mind rested on what I wanted for Java. I wanted Java to feel good about herself, to be able to cope with stress, to make better choices, and to find a way to help reduce the size and intensity of her fearful 'whale eyes'.

It seemed like I had already tried so much with her but something wasn't clicking for both of us. Her aggressive behavior wasn't going to get better quickly with the wave of my wand or anyone else's wand. Eager to do whatever I could to help, I had already enrolled in an aggression-reduction workshop to be presented by Patricia McConnell in three weeks.

On Monday morning, my first day back at work after my Chicago experience, I bubbled with excitement about the Tellington TTouch® workshop to my friend and colleague, Alana. Listening attentively and seeing the passion sparkle brightly in my eyes, Alana informed me quite firmly that I absolutely *must* attend. We no sooner finished our conversation and she shuffled me off to see Ann, the school principal.

"Go right now and tell Ann you want to take your personal days to attend the workshop. You need to go. This opportunity won't happen again," said Alana with the force of a true friend, and the spirit of a guardian angel.

Walking toward Ann's office, my mind tried to change itself, even though she already knew how passionate I was about wanting to work with kids and animals together.

How can I tell my principal and boss of eight years that I want to stop teaching the future of America so I can pet animals for a living?

"Hey, can I come in?" I knocked quietly, and smiled apprehensively.

Greeting me inside the wide-open door was Ann's warm smile which welcomed me quickly, and her gentle demeanor that eased me completely.

"Of course. Have a seat. You want some candy?" Ann asked as she passed me a bowl of heavenly chocolates.

As I sat down and unwrapped the gold and blue metallic wrapper on my bite size bar, my heart pounded with delight and anticipation.

"You know how much I *love* working with kids," I started out factually, "and you know how much I *love* being around animals," I continued, as an emotional lump entered quickly into my throat, reminding me about my heartfelt passion, "I want to work with both some day and I need to pursue something in order to see if I can make that happen," I told Ann as she nodded her head back in validation. "There's a five-day animal training happening in Minneapolis in a few weeks, but I'd need to take a few days off of school to make it happen, and...."

"Do it!" Ann smiled widely with small tears forming in her eyes, then threw her arms around me in the most fantastic embrace of acceptance and support.

Before the school day was over, I signed up for the TTouch Foundation Training for Companion Animals.

Journal Entry
4/1/02 - Path

I just scheduled my hotel and am sending in my final payment for the TTouch Training! I'm excited and nervous lots of money and time with Java—hoping it'll all be good. But for now, I'm just grateful that she's come into my life so that I can be pushed to pursue my dream.   "I'm going to figure out a way to make money petting animals." Where we can be in a year's time—wow! My journey of working with my heart and hands has begun!

Because of Java, I was searching. I was searching for a method that worked well for her, and also felt right to me. TTouch seemed like something that was definitely worth trying, and now I had the support to make it happen. Java and I seemed to be in a holding pattern because I was unsure what kind of training to do and what *not* to do. I didn't want

93

to wreck anything we'd already done, yet I didn't know what else was possible.

A few weeks later, I attended Patricia McConnell's two-day workshop on aggression-reduction. She is a gifted and entertaining speaker, and unbelievably knowledgeable about dogs and the people who love them. It was absolutely wonderful and filled me with hope, ideas, and tons of valuable information. At the end of the first day, I talked briefly with Patricia about Java, and told her that I was attending my first Tellington TTouch® Training in a month to see how that felt. She was very supportive and reminded me that it takes a special person to continue to work with a challenging dog in a smart and safe manner.

Two days of learning and understanding about why dogs snarl and what you can do to help them left me feeling very optimistic. Over the next couple of weeks, Java and I spent a lot of time approaching spooky things with a pack of hot dogs. As a vegetarian, I think hot dogs are spooky, so even *buying* them was a personal victory for me.

Off with our hot dogs we went each day, down the street, up the block and into my local vet's office so the receptionist could help Java get past one of her many fears. We continued down the block, passing the scary soda machine from the opposite side of the street, then the middle of the street and finally the same side of the street. This took weeks. Hot dog, hot dog, hot dog. Spooky red, white and blue flag waving in the breeze? Hot dog. Super spooky man limping down the sidewalk with glasses, a beard and a baseball hat? Many hot dogs.

Soon, Java began to nudge me when something challenging was coming near, as if to reassure herself that the hot dogs were still there, or that I was. In no time at all, Java was telling *me* when she needed them. Although she was able to take hot dogs from complete strangers with less fear in her eyes, and pass soda machines and flags with less tension in her body, she was still scared. So was I.

Our TTouch workshop in Minnesota was only a week away. My thoughts turned to curiosity about whether this 'no fear, no force' type of work was for real and hoped that it would do the trick for Java and I. Even just planning the trip brought anxiety to me, as Java had never ridden in the car for more than half an hour. She'd certainly never stayed in a hotel and hadn't been around large groups of dogs and people for long periods of time.

A trip to Minneapolis meant about a five-hour car ride, five full days in a classroom setting and five nights in a hotel. We would be together non-stop for about 130 hours. I already felt like a prisoner and we hadn't even left yet!

While packing for our trip, I felt guilty about leaving Clio behind with Rebecca for six days. Her health was failing and there were times she'd forget where she was and sort of daze out in the back yard. Other times, she'd run for the patio door and run right into it, shaking her body and looking around in hopes that nobody else noticed. Although leaving Clio was difficult, I felt relieved to know she'd be in good hands so I'd be able to give my full attention to Java for the first time ever.

Emotionally, I was very anxious about money. I was paying $500 for the training, an extra $700 for hotels and food, and taking three unpaid days off of work.

Could I really afford to go?
Could I really afford not to go?

Financial worry sucks. What I realized was that in order to follow my heart, I needed to overcome some fear. I had learned how to pray, surrender, have faith, and allow my friends, family and colleagues to coax me through that last, little, scary bit. Who *hasn't* ever been worried about money? Sometimes when you know you need to leap, you just do it and hope for the best. I've never regretted any of the leaps I've made in my life because when you stop to look fear in the face, great things happen.

The morning of our trip, I explained to Clio where Java and I were going (and why), then dropped her off at Rebecca's, explaining further why she was being left behind. The calm look in her eyes assured me she was grateful to be left behind. Once I got back home to load the car, I laughed at how difficult it can be to pack for a dog. It's almost harder than packing for a human! Dog crate, dog food, dog dishes, dog treats, dog leashes, dog vet records, dog poop bags, dog. The car looked and smelled like I knew what I was doing. With Java strapped into the back seat of my black SUV, and me strapped into the front, I turned around and smiled.

"Here we go, Little Brown Bear," I said, as I reached back and touched her chest. I didn't know what else to say, or expect.

The rhythmic bumps on the interstate lulled Java into a deep sleep for the entire ride. Now I understand why my parents told me they kept driving when my sister and I were napping. You don't dare stop. When we reached the hotel, it was a whole different story. Gathering as much dog stuff as I could in one arm, I took the leashed dog in the other. Down the long, carpeted hallway we trotted, with Java sniffing and pulling like a dog on the hot trail of a fabulous scent. I don't think hotels smell very good, but maybe they do to dogs. At the end of the hall, near the exit, was our simple, little room.

Two double beds stood out like a party waiting to happen, all dolled up in the most horrid quilt I've ever seen. I was exhausted already and hoped Java still was, too.

Unclipping her leash, I no more than started to unpack our stuff and she lunged violently at herself in the mirrors—attacking the likeness but not understanding it was only her own reflection snarling back at her. She also lunged and barked at the door every time shadows of feet passed by in the light, which happens quite frequently in a hotel. Then, she spent until five a.m. woofing at every little creaky squeak or spooky spook that dared enough to make a noise at that odd hour. When I tried to find enough privacy and solace to shower, she tried to rip the shower curtain down to ease her anxiety, so I showered without privacy.

Needless to say, I arrived at the first day of my workshop a nervous wreck and near tears with an overstressed Plott Hound attached at my hip. I guess it must have been obvious. Within moments of our arrival, it was like a professional orchestra was being directed. Someone held Java, someone set up my crate, someone handed me a pen and told me to sign some papers, and someone looked me right in the eye and immediately touched my heart with hers.

Edie Jane.

Wispy grey curls and a thick Canadian accent, Edie Jane Eaton was like a motherly ray of sunshine. As the instructor for the week, Edie Jane poetically and strategically situated herself right next to Java and I in the large circle of chairs. More people joined the circle and more dogs, and I found myself feeling incredibly nervous and substantially inadequate. Concerned about how Java might react, I held the leash tightly in my hand, held my breath, and hoped for the best. Java lunged and snarled, and I felt embarrassed and became paralyzed. Java lunged and snarled, and I made excuses. Java lunged and snarled, and Edie Jane smiled at me then gently took the leash out of my hand. In that very moment, I felt love and compassion like never before—and relief.

"She's only a bit scared, that's all," Edie Jane said to me, then looked down at Java. "Come on, girl. Let's get you feeling a little better about yourself."

Journal Entry
5/1/02 - TTouch Training: Session 1, Day 1

Java has violent, aggressive behavior and stares at the other dogs until she blows up like a cannon—lunging, flailing and showing her teeth. It takes her forever to stop panting and come back to normal.

What am I getting myself into? There are 15 dogs and 18 people here! How are we going to get through five full days of this? I'm already frustrated.

Edie Jane took Java across the room to see how she'd do away from me. Java walked about six feet, turned around and barreled her way into my lap and put her arms around my neck. Her reactions were really strong today—a lot of staring at other dogs, then lunging forward and snapping. Edie Jane changed her leash and put on a Body Wrap and some other equipment but I was on edge and frustrated. Java fell asleep snoring on my shoe in the afternoon and her legs were really tight. By the end of the day, her tail was wagging a lot more and she was starting to approach people with more confidence and less apprehension. She's still barking at sounds but she was able to walk past two dogs in the parking lot without a hard glance from thirty feet away.

With the wave of her special TTouch wand, Edie Jane whisked Java off to the dressing room for a quick makeover. Java returned to the circle wearing a brand new, color-coordinated costume that matched her fur perfectly.

A dark brown step-in harness, tan Halti® head collar, and black, leather double-ended leash made Java look like a brindle biker chick with an attitude. One end of the double-ended leash was clipped underneath Java's muzzle on the head collar, and the other end of the leash was clipped to the ring right behind her shoulders on the step-in harness. Connected to the leash, was Miss Edie Jane at the helm. If you've ever handed your dog over to someone else, a challenging dog like Java, you know exactly how I was feeling—responsible.

While Java stood in balance by her side, Edie Jane explained how Java lacked self-control and didn't have the correct calming signals to tell other dogs she was afraid. In other words, she stared at dogs, unable to make herself look away, until she felt so frightened that she lunged at them. The head collar was to help steer her head away from staring at another dog, and the harness around her chest was to help bring her body back into balance when she lunged forward. Java lunged, and I held my breath, then looked at Edie Jane and smiled. Java's lunging was easily managed with this equipment and a handler who knew what she was doing.

Within minutes, Java was easily learning how to turn her head away and bring her body back into balance with less and less guidance. She was already learning how to make her own positive choices and change some habits she had become accustomed to. As for me, I was watching carefully—trying to figure out how on earth I was going to maneuver a leash in each hand and still walk my reactive dog while carrying a hot cup of coffee!

Later in the morning, Edie Jane added another simple piece of equipment to Java's wardrobe—a TTouch Half Body Wrap. The Body Wrap was a three-inch elastic bandage that wrapped around Java's body in a figure eight pattern—creating a sort of 'hug' around her body. The purpose of the Body Wrap was to help Java feel more secure so she could focus on what she was doing with her body.

For what seemed like hours, Java's behavior served as a teaching moment for the entire class. Inside, I felt a strange combination of pride and embarrassment, but Edie Jane showed me quickly, easily, and gently how capable Java was. My heart grew in leaps and bounds as I watched Java settle, think, and balance herself with the help of Edie Jane.

Understanding another being completely isn't always an easy undertaking. Java was capable of a lot more than I was aware, and so was I. Sometime during the morning of our first TTouch Training a shift took place when I finally witnessed Java's true potential around other dogs. Java felt it in herself for the first time as well, and we both learned she was very capable with the right tools to assist her.

With class ready to resume after lunch, Edie Jane perched Java quietly on her right side, and continued to hold her leash loosely. Up to this point, this was one of the few times I was able to be near my dog while casually drinking a hot cup of coffee. What I also learned quickly is that you can't really pay proper attention to a reactive dog when you're busy paying attention to your coffee. The other dogs and humans began to rejoin the circle after lunch, and I could sense Java's cork ready to pop at any moment. I took in a long, deep breath, as Edie Jane turned and smiled at me—reminding me to also exhale. With a gentle pat on my leg she reassured me with her sweet, soothing voice.

"You're doing fine. So is Miss Java," she said, as she began to do circular TTouches on Java's shoulder.

Java looked at Edie Jane, and acknowledged the woman who was on the other end of the hand that was making her feel so nice. Looking away, Java's eyes quickly connected with a pit bull mix across the circle. She held her gaze and I held my breath.

Lightning fast, I felt Java's energy shift and her whole body begin to stiffen. Like a Canadian TTouch samurai, Edie Jane turned swiftly to Java, broke her hard gaze by steering her head away, and tapped her ever so gently on top of her head.

"Think about it, girl," Edie Jane said firmly to Java.

"Yeah, right," I thought to myself, but she did! Java turned her head away from the other dog all by herself and looked into Edie Jane's eyes, and heart. From that moment forward, I believed wholeheartedly in Tellington TTouch® Training.

Journal Entry
5/2/02 - TTouch Training: Session 1, Day 2

Edie Jane convinced me to board Java at the nearby kennel so I could get some sleep. I'm glad! When I picked her up this morning, she was wild to see me but then we worked on walking slow together with her new harness and leash. It worked! She barked at one of the women in the class, but then approached her and wagged her tail. Later in the day, she got really agitated and was more reactive to other dogs without her Body Wrap, so I put it back on. It's amazing to me what a difference such a simple tool makes with her! By lunchtime, she was wagging at dogs from afar. I'm still amazed how apparent the anxiety is in her eyes and how little I used to notice. She's working so hard. Bless her heart.

Journal Entry
5/3/02 - TTouch Training: Session 1, Day 3

Java is exhausted. So am I. She worked with other handlers in the class today for the first time—working in the Confidence Course/Playground for Higher Learning to help her with coordination, balance and posture. Watching Java from afar helps me to see her anxiety more easily, and also how I influence it by watching her and/or encouraging her. At the same time, it's also really beautiful to see the love that other people have for her, too. I was amazed how well she did. She can actually move slowly and pay attention!

Today we learned how to do circular TTouches, lifts and slides: Zig Zag, Raccoon, Chimp, Bear, Abalone, Hair Slides, Ear TTouches, Clouded Leopard, Lying Leopard, Python Lifts and Llama.

We're learning how to give direction to an animal instead of correction, to use our voices in a neutral way and praise good behavior. We've learned about using two points of contact to help an animal with balance and self-control—using a collar/head collar and a harness with a double ended leash. (Java got to demonstrate that!) We also learned how to start working with cats. This work is really amazing!

Journal Entry
5/4/02 - TTouch Training: Session 1, Day 4

Java did GREAT this morning! She made smart choices around other dogs and is starting to break her gaze on her own. She started the day by lying on the floor, chewing a bone, and I let her run off leash in a secluded field at break. We experienced some nice, quiet time alone this morning before class and it seemed to help. I'm super proud of her!!

By the fourth day, I was a different woman. With only twenty-one hours of training under my belt, I had relaxed, and Java had relaxed. I had also accepted the fact that it was okay to kennel Java at night, so I could actually get some sleep and focus the next day. Other people in the class were finally starting to take her leash so I could go to the bathroom in peace. I felt an understanding that I hadn't had before, and a gentle softness began to appear within my heart. For once, I felt like a part of a group who understood, accepted, and supported both Java and I.

"Alright, I want each of you to go find a quiet spot and spend fifteen minutes doing TTouches with your dogs," announced Edie Jane, as she shuffled us off to practice and process what we'd learned.

Do you have any idea how hard it is to walk across a training room filled with dogs and humans, trying to maneuver a reactive dog on a double-ended leash while carrying a blanket? So much for the cup of coffee!

We settled into our semi-private spot along the perimeter of the training room. Laying out our dark green, fleece blanket, I scanned the room, and noticed that everyone else was already sitting down and working with their dogs. Java and I were just getting situated. Looking up at me with a tan, head collar draped loosely over her muzzle, Java's soft eyes connected with mine. It felt like the first time in days where I was able to look at her. Sitting down on the blanket, I patted the space next to me and smiled. She was calm and so was I. With plenty of space between us and the next dog/human team, I took off Java's head collar and harness and re-clipped her leash to her collar—giving her some freedom from her new costume. Java rubbed her naked muzzle against my shoulder with joy, then flopped her body onto the fuzzy, green blanket—looking back at me in appreciation.

Big, deep, human exhale. Big, deep, canine sigh.

With a gentle, quiet space in my heart, I started touching Java's body with a long, slow, full body stroke called Noah's March. Java watched my hand closely as it traveled carefully across the dips, hills and valleys of her strong, dense frame, and I felt the temperature shift beneath the palm of my hand as I moved to different parts of her body. Warm heart, cold feet. I started to become aware of the elasticity of the skin around her neck, head and chest, and the tension in her legs, hindquarters, and tail. Java's eyes softened, as she wiggled on her blanket, sighed, then looked over at the next human/dog duo engaged in the same love game. I think she felt lucky. I did.

Shifting my hands for the Lying Leopard TTouch, I began to do some slow, circular TTouches on Java's shoulder, moving the skin in a clockwise circle and a quarter beneath the pads of my fingers. I felt my own body relax a bit more and watched Java's do the same. It was like a sensual dance we had agreed to do together yet no one was leading because no one had to. Beautiful, slow, sensual, connected, love, understanding. Java gave a huge exhale, finally laid her entire body down on the blanket, then peered up at me with soft eyes.

Her breathing slowed to a normal pace, and the skin on her body didn't feel quite as tight as it had earlier in the day. Practicing the Ear TTouches I had learned, I felt the warmth of her velvety, brown ears between my thumb and index finger as I stroked down the full length of her ear—paying attention to each detail. Java and I relaxed into the moment even more, and it felt as if nothing in the world existed except for us. Changing to a Clouded Leopard TTouch, I worked these tiny circles down the side of her strong neck, onto her right shoulder and continued down the side of her strong, brindle body with a pressure as light as if I were working on a baby bird. Java sighed and turned her head slowly to look at me with her sweet, chestnut-brown eyes. Noticing her soft gaze, I rested my hand gently over her heart and paused into the peace of the moment.

What came next, was a feeling that's difficult to explain but absolutely amazing to experience. In that very moment, when Java's eyes met mine, our souls locked so deeply it was as if a special agreement had just taken place. My heartstrings played a sweet and gentle chord, and for what seemed like the first time ever, I truly saw who she was—a soft, tender, misunderstood being. Warm tears fell in small puddles down my cheeks as Java and I looked softly through loving eyes at one another. Then I began to apologize straight from my heart to hers.

I apologized for forcing her, scaring her, for not knowing, and not understanding. Java cocked her head from left to right as I continued to apologize for yelling at her, swatting her, tugging at her, confusing her, questioning her, and judging her. I finally felt like I understood. Java, having never broken her gaze throughout my entire apology, leaned her sweet head forward, licked the salty tears gently from my face, then forgave completely.

"I didn't know, girl. I'm so, so sorry."

Turning my head to wipe a tear from my eye, I noticed one of my classmates nearby. Watching the private interaction between Java and I, she wiped the tears from her own eyes, then whispered to me,

"You two are really lucky to have each other."

We were. We are.

Our five-day training came to a close at the end of the following day, as each of us shared our personal stories and achievements from the week. Looking around the circle, I noticed beautiful changes in other people and animals as well. Java was sound asleep—snoring—on her fuzzy, green blanket behind me, while I waited for the right time to share.

What lessons had I learned?
Did I know these people well enough to share my heart?
What if I started to cry?

I waited for what seemed like an eternity for everyone else to share, and then Java made me do it. Stretching gallantly from her hideout behind my chair, Java awakened slowly yet confidently from her nap. Her scheme seemed quite obvious. Stretching her sleepy body again as she walked around my chair, Java turned once to glance back at me out of the corner of her eye and kept going—right into the middle of the circle. For Java, it was the first of many very bold moves and I knew it was a sign. This time, I paid attention to the sign and followed the nudge at the end of the leash.

"Well, I guess we're next," I said sheepishly.

I took a big breath and recalled the date. May 5, 2002. "Two years ago tomorrow, I was in a pretty bad car accident...."

Tears already. Breathe.

Staring at the off-white linoleum floor below, I waited to catch myself. Out of the corner of my eye was my Little Brown Bear—standing stoically at my left side—her soulful eyes peering at me sideways as if to coax me on. I could hear words of cheer and praise in her glance.

Go on. Tell em' the truth. I'm here.

Reaching down, I gave Java a gentle stroke on the right side of her muzzle, then took a deep breath. Tears fell peacefully down my cheeks, as I thanked her profusely for teaching me so much during the week. Java's deep, brown eyes connected easily with mine, then pierced through my heart. I lost it.

This is really hard for me to cry in front of new people.

Most of my life I spent crying alone, or not crying at all. This time, Java stood next to me, like a rock, ready to support no matter what fell out of my mouth. Java's strength and our special bond radiated throughout the room as I started to hear a few other people sniffling, too. Misery loves company.

"...I realized through my car accident that I was saved for a reason. That reason was to open my heart, and I've been given another chance. I want to use my heart and hands in my work, and I found out this week that TTouch is it for me. Thank you, girl," I said, as I looked deep into Java's soft, chestnut eyes and sobbed freely. So did everyone else.

A stillness fell over the room and only one more person remained to speak. Kelly kept quiet the entire week, and she had also intrigued me all week. With her tall, wiry body and long, brown and red streaked hair covering her face, she seemed to be as afraid of the world as Java and I were. There's something about an immediate kinship when you can feel and understand another person's strength and suffering by observing them. That's how it was with Kelly from the beginning. I knew we were going to become great friends as Kelly closed out our circle with her quick and quiet commentary about how much she loved TTouch, too.

Hugs abounded as everyone packed up their belongings to head home. As the room emptied out, Java and I looked exhausted yet we were both vibrating with new energy. Moving over to pack up Java's crate, I felt someone walk up behind me, and as I turned around slowly, I smiled. It was Edie Jane. We hugged as if we'd known each other forever, then I thanked her for all of her help with Java during the week, and all she'd done for me personally. She smiled back with gratitude in her face, then knelt down toward the hound by my side, and gave her complete attention to Miss Java.

"Goodbye, sweet Angel Pie," Edie Jane whispered gently into Java's ear, then added a loving touch under her velvety, brown muzzle.

A wet kiss from Java gave Edie Jane the Plott Hound seal of approval. Java and I drove home from that trip as changed beings, with a much closer bond and a better understanding of each other and ourselves. She slept the entire ride home, while my body buzzed with excitement. Turning into Rebecca's driveway, I couldn't wait to see Clio and share some stories of our adventures. Java and I hopped out of the car, stretched our legs, then headed inside to fetch Clio.

Java was absolutely thrilled to see her, proving it so by licking her muzzle—throwing Clio's head back each time in what seemed like a violent love affair. Clio stood still and listened patiently as Java told the same stories over and over, and over.

Work seemed different when I returned the next day. I felt disconnected—like I'd experienced something secretive and special. I had. As I shared my thoughts and stories with my colleagues, there was a strong feeling that something had changed. Me. Two days later, I phoned the Tellington TTouch® office in Santa Fe, New Mexico to commit to a two-year program. I was on my way to becoming a Certified Tellington TTouch Practitioner for Companion Animals.

CHAPTER SEVEN

GRATITUDE

"The secret of happiness

is not found in seeking more,

but in developing the capacity to enjoy less."

~ Dan Millman

Stuff was happening in my heart, alright. In just five short days I learned how to understand both humans and animals better by watching, feeling, letting go and letting love exude from the core of my being. I learned to accept and love Java for who she was, and where she was, instead of wanting her to be different. In one simple moment by the wall when we looked deeply into each other's souls, and she licked the tears from my face, my heart grew to a place of gratitude.

Gratitude is really simple when you think about all the things in your life that are going well. It's quite manageable to be grateful for the easy parts. But the place where the most growth occurs is finding gratitude in the challenging parts — those little rocks along the way that you want to toss back long before you're willing to notice that they're gems in disguise. It's much simpler to stomp your feet and wish for things to be different than to be grateful for all of the opportunities you have in your life.

I kept a gratitude journal for years — writing down five things I was grateful for every morning. Some days, it was easy to come up with five. Other days, I really had to struggle. Within time, I learned that gratitude comes in the most special wrapping and it's our task to uncover it, explore it and celebrate it. Gratitude is a special gift that can be found in countless opportunities throughout each and every day.

Don't you like presents? I do!

Over the next two weeks I practiced everything I learned — how to do circular TTouches to help calm an animal, and how to guide a dog instead of force them. Most of all, I learned how to be aware, listen, respect, and truly pay attention. I began to think more like an animal instead of a human. My life was settling into a different place and I was unbelievably excited about my new path of working with animals. I knew in my heart I'd teach art in the public schools for another two years, if that, but hoped I'd find a way to work with kids and animals some day in the future.

This animal work really grabbed my soul and I loved every part of it, wanting to pursue it as a career. As an added bonus, I started to love myself in the process. I felt as if I'd come to a glorious place of peace and calm in my life—letting go of relationships that needed letting go of, and mending relationships that needed mending.

My relationship with my Dad was one that I'd worked hard to mend over the years, and I was grateful to have done so. After he and my Mom divorced when I was a teenager, he moved to Costa Rica. For twenty years of my life, and his, he spent his time in a house near the ocean, selling various pieces of used equipment to various strangers.

My Dad could sell bananas to monkeys. He was like a whimsical cartoon character, and it took me a long time to accept him for who he was, and love him anyway. When I was a teenager, I was really angry with him, but as an adult, I finally realized how important it was to make amends.

My Dad and I got a lot closer after my divorce. We emailed about once a week and often phoned each other about once a month to catch up or hear each other's voices. We only saw each other once a year if we were lucky, and I was really missing him when I picked up the phone that night.

It was almost two weeks after Java and I had returned from our TTouch Training—May 17, 2002—as a tiny snippet of my life became etched in my mind and heart forever. I was hanging out in the kitchen, making a veggie pizza and dancing to steamy Latin music—one of my favorite pastimes—when the urge to call my Dad rose from my heart to my fingertips. While pretending I was adept at salsa dancing while simultaneously chopping red peppers, I waited for his low voice to answer.

"Hey Dad! How are you?" I asked with a big smile on my face, and an even bigger smile in my heart.

"Hey, baby. I'm good. What a nice surprise!" he replied gently but with excitement.

I could feel him smiling, yet his voice sounded different. It was wavering.

"What are you up to?" he continued on—his once low voice sounded clear and changed after quitting his nearly fifty-year smoking habit.

"I'm heading out to meet some friends in a bit. We're going to see some live music. I was making a pizza and thinking of you, and I just wanted to call and say hi, that's all," I said, smiling deeply inside.

With little hesitation, he replied, "When are you coming to visit?"

"As soon as my passport comes in the mail, Dad. I checked on flights today and it looks like I can get there the middle or end of June," I replied, then asked with concern, "Dad, are you okay?"

"Well, they want to do surgery. I'm scared."

I'd never heard my father utter those two words: I'm scared. I listened as he told me how the doctors wanted to remove the malignant tumor they found in his bladder a month earlier.

"I'm not having surgery." His big, boomy voice sounded weaker than I'd ever noticed.

He *was* afraid.

"Dad, I'll be there as soon as I can. I promise." We chatted a little more about basic stuff you talk to your Dad about, then we etched our closing in stone.

"I love you, Dad," I beamed.

"I love you too, baby," he beamed back.

Click.

My Dad died unexpectedly eleven days later, and my passport arrived in the mail the following day. When someone you love dies suddenly, all you can do is replay those last moments over and over to make sure it's all okay, and to try to make sense of it all.

There was a sort of surreal feeling about the night he passed on. It was a Tuesday and it had been raining most of the day. Moments before I went to sleep that night, I lay in bed praying for others and asking for guidance for myself—my nightly bedtime ritual at that time in my life. Lightning flashed and thunder crashed as Java rested easily in her usual puffy chair in the living room, and Clio snoozed peacefully in her chosen bed in my office.

While sending prayers of good health to my Dad, his wife, and my little half-sisters, a *huge* crack of thunder broke, as lightning lit up my entire bedroom. The next thing I remembered was the sound of the answering machine waking me up an hour later. It was 11:10.

Calls at night are creepy. Running through the darkness to answer the phone, I heard my Dad's wife, Gioconda, on the answering machine. She was shouting for me to wake up, as I was scurrying toward the rectangular box with the blinking red light in the living room.

"Gioco?" I asked, as an eerie pause filled the dark spaces in my house, and froze the moment in stillness.

"Your Daddy has passed on," she said slowly, quietly and with excruciating pain in her voice that I'll never forget.

A barrage of questions filled my mind and I felt the blood in my body rise to the surface of my skin in disbelief. A massive heart attack had taken my Dad a few hours earlier—around the time I was praying for him. My mind scanned quickly for any shred of understanding and I rested gently on the closing words of our last phone conversation.

I love you, Dad. I love you too, baby.

The middle of the night can be the loneliest and spookiest time. A sudden heaviness filled my entire house as I hung up the phone, while both dogs remained sound asleep. I felt completely alone—unsure of what to do and what not to do. I reminded myself of my mother's wisdom, ("When in doubt, don't.") then paced impatiently until the answers presented themselves.

Should I call my mother to tell her that her ex-husband died suddenly and let her stay awake all night? Should I call my sister in Arizona?

I paced for awhile to find some clarity, then finally picked up the phone to call my friend, Rachelle. She had recently lost her mother, and I knew she'd understand. Only true friends answer the phone after midnight. Completely dumbstruck, I told her my news, then waited for some sort of comforting response. Without a hitch in her voice, she asked softly and sweetly,

"What's the best thing about your father?"

"His smile," I responded quickly and easily. Then, I stopped pacing, and smiled myself.

We talked until I felt safe enough to be alone in my house, then we hung up. While Java and Clio continued to sleep peacefully, I phoned my sister, Stephanie. She wasn't home, so all I could do was tell her husband the news and ask him to have Steph call me as soon as possible. I felt trapped. Stephanie was speaking at a conference in California and wouldn't be available for a few hours. Right then I needed the patience I didn't have. I was concerned for how hard my sister would take the news since she and my Dad had struggled to have a harmonious relationship for years. I hung up the phone and walked slowly into the living room and sat down. I felt numb.

Noticing a family heirloom resting solidly on my shelf, I walked over and picked up the ceramic menorah and set it on my coffee table in front of the big, picture window in the living room. I wondered if it was sacrilegious to light the entire menorah—especially on May 28 instead of Hanukkah. It didn't matter.

A quiet place of stillness filled me as I lit all nine candles, then prayed for my Dad's soul harder than I'd ever prayed in my life. I prayed for those he had betrayed to forgive him, for those who had loved him to find peace, and I prayed that he had experienced peace and love at the end of his life. I sat until the last of the candles flickered out and only the smell of wax and tiny trails of smoke remained.

Sleepy Java joined me lazily in the living room, curling her warm body into mine. Lying beside her, I kissed her short fur and told her how much I loved her, and how grateful I was to have her in my life. Then I told her about my Dad. Java and I laid in stillness for a long while, surrounded by scents of wax and smoke, creating memories in the middle of the night.

Riiinnnnngggg!!!

The phone startled me out of a deep trance. Walking slowly to pick it up, Java turned sleepily to watch. I knew it was Stephanie. On the other end of the line, I heard my sister crying harder than I'd ever heard before.

"I was gonna call him," she said, between uncontrollable sobs.

My heart ached for her. I listened through her tears at the regret and disbelief she seemed to be feeling in that moment, and after a short while, she caught her breath and paused.

"Why are you so calm?" Stephanie asked curiously.

"I'm really not sure. I guess I must be at peace," I responded quietly, as I looked out the living room window at the tops of the trees against the night sky.

Stephanie and I talked for over an hour—trying to find resolution together about the death of our father. The physical distance between us tugged at my heart when I couldn't reach out to give her a hug. Neither one of us wanted to hang up, yet both of us were exhausted. The world seemed completely silent while the moon cast long shadows of trees that stretched across the street. As Stephanie and I said our good nights, I crawled back into bed, next to Java, who'd secretly stolen my place.

The next morning, I woke up in a complete daze and wondered if the phone call was real since everything seemed surreal. Then I geared up for the toughest call—my mother. Phoning her, I took a deep breath and waited for her always joyous voice to answer the phone. Telling myself to be strong, I heard my Mom pick up the other end of the line, and I lost it. There's something about hearing your mother's voice that takes away all of the filters you use to try to masquerade your emotions.

"It's me," I said slowly as my voice wavered.

"Honey, what is it?" she asked lovingly.

"Dad died."

I'll never forget the huge gasp of air my Mom took in when I told her the news. She and my Dad were married almost twenty years, and for almost another twenty years, they were divorced. Having been divorced myself, I understand the bond you create with someone you spend so much time with. Sudden news of a loved one dying hits you hard no matter what the past entailed.

Hanging up the phone, I readied myself and walked to work in a fog. There wasn't much I could do except continue on with my life that day. I felt numb inside and also worried because I hadn't cried yet, but somehow I felt peaceful and okay with it. To this day, our final 'I love you' continues to echo in my heart, but as much deep gratitude as I feel for the last great conversation I had with my Dad, nothing prepares you for the sudden loss of a parent. It took me three days after my Dad died to feel the effects of having lost him so suddenly. It's taken years afterward to grieve fully, and I still miss him like crazy.

Journal Entry
5/30/02 - My Daddy

My Daddy could sell bananas to monkeys. His wide smile and sea green eyes filled any room. His voice, so boomy and low that changed with time, became mellower and calmer — less filled with the nicotine of Pall Mall non-filters.

The songs he sang to me — Old Man River *and* Sunrise, Sunset *from the times of being a small child going to bed, calmed me and lulled me to sleep by the soothing bass voice of Daddy.*

My Daddy made me laugh repeatedly, like a cartoon character changing over and over. Generous with love, always. A heart of gold and a heart filled with pain and fear.

My Daddy ruled the ocean. Floating. Most at peace on the water, selling bananas to monkeys, or water to fish.

I cried, laughed, smiled, danced, reminisced and tried to figure out how to grieve while living alone. I felt isolated with my animal work, and now with my Dad being gone, I felt even more like a part of me had been ripped out. My Dad and I had become really close and it hurt horribly to have him gone.

Then my life became more challenging. Six days after my Dad died, I came home from work to find Clio completely paralyzed from the waist down. Lying on the couch in her own feces and urine, she was unable to wag her tail to show

how glad she felt that I was finally home. Clio looked at me through eyes that only an animal lover who has lost an animal would recognize. I felt horrible wondering how long she had been lying there and felt the end very near. I ran to let Java out of her crate, then she bounced all over the house, and bounced her way over to give Clio a kiss. Clio's head rocked backwards from the force behind the smooch, and Java, for the first time ever, kept all four feet on the ground instead of jumping all over Clio and I. She knew, too.

I called Clio's regular vet on the far side of Madison, then called my local vet who was only two blocks away. Cleaning Clio up, I told Java I needed to focus only on Clio for awhile—that she was sick and I needed her (Java) to be a big girl, which translated as "please settle down because I can't handle any more right now."

My local vet was fabulous. Dave was a big, burly guy with a heart twice the size of the sun, and equally warm and soothing. He worked with Veta, Clio and Java on various occasions and we'd built up a really nice relationship over the years. When I told him about Clio's sudden decline, he asked me point blank if she needed help in passing on. I knew she wasn't ready. Giving me his home phone number just in case, I hung up and called Rebecca in tears.

"It's Clio."

She was at my door in six minutes. Rebecca and I laid on the floor together, talked, cried and wondered about the right thing to do. Clio's eyes were absolutely lit up with life, yet her body was limp and lifeless. I moved her slippery body to the floor, situated a plastic garbage bag under her rear, and covered the rest of her frail, black body with a colorful, fleece blanket. Java laid quietly on the couch the entire time—watching, feeling, and settling, just as I had requested.

Rebecca went home after about an hour, and my house was filled with a density I can't explain. When an animal is in transition, the energy in the house shifts. Java knew, Clio knew the end was near, and I knew, and now it was only a matter of time. I slept in the living room all night, next to Clio, with my hand on her chest so I could feel her rib cage expand and exhale. Java kept a close watch over both of us from her perch on the puffy, yellow chair.

Morning came and Clio wasn't any better, or any worse. Her eyes looked like she was ready to get up and go but her body wasn't able to respond. Calling my principal in tears, I took the day off of work and spent most of it doing some of the circular TTouches I learned only four weeks earlier. What I knew then was that the circular TTouches helped to reduce stress and calm an animal, and I wanted Clio's transition to be as relaxing as possible. Java, Clio and I spent the entire day less than two feet from one another—sharing Chinese food, telling stories, laughing, touching, crying, remembering, and grieving.

At about 2:30 I phoned my sister, Stephanie, to figure out when and if to make the difficult decision to euthanize Clio. As an animal lover herself, Stephanie was not only my older sister, she was also a great source of wisdom to me. She still is.

"How do her eyes look?" asked Stephanie, while I looked at Clio attentively.

"They look fi..." I began, then stopped.

From across the room, I was about to witness a beautiful gift. Clio looked back at me, then opened her mouth wider than a yawn, into a contortion I had never witnessed before.

"Steph, hang on. I think she's dying. Something's happening!"

Like a swift summer breeze floating across warm skin, I watched Clio's invisible exhale turn into a milky, white vapor that extended out about six inches into space. It happened twice in a row.

"Steph, I've gotta go," I said, as I hung up the phone and looked closely into Clio's eyes.

A glassy, dull look in her eyes showed me that her spirit released, but her body was still holding on. With a big exhale and a heavy heart, I called Dr. Dave to tell him I needed help with Clio's passing.

Hanging up the phone, I looked over at Clio who was lying limp on a black garbage bag and a blanket on the floor, then over at Java who was full of life and practicing self-control on the couch. Java jumped quickly off the couch, stretched her whole body out, walked confidently over to Clio, and licked her once on the muzzle. Then she walked directly into her kennel, sat down, and waited for me to latch the door so I could take Clio away forever.

Who says animals don't feel?

Dialing the phone again, I waited for my dear friend, Mara, to answer.

"I need help with Clio," I said quietly and in tears.

"I'll be right there."

When an animal is paralyzed and you're getting ready to euthanize them, that shouldn't be the least bit humorous. But two grown women trying to make a doggie hammock out of a grey and white blanket, and do it with straight faces, is very difficult. Especially if one of those faces is Mara's. With the vet's office only two blocks away, we could've made a great spectacle in a small town by carrying Clio through the streets in her doggie hammock, but we didn't.

With a few small giggles, we hoisted Clio's homemade hammock out the door, down the walkway, and into the back of my SUV. Then, we did the same in reverse once we got to the vet's office. I'm sure they'd seen everything, but in retrospect it must have looked a bit strange. For Clio, a queen's procession wasn't out of the question. We rushed Clio through the waiting room, and into the back room to rest her gently on the stainless steel, rectangular table.

Dr. Dave checked Clio's vitals, then tried to find any signal of strong reflexes from her. Clio's entire body showed signs of weakness, and also the strength of being ready to let go.

"Are you sure you're ready for this?" he asked, as he explained that Clio was failing quickly.

"Yep. And I want to stay with her," I replied firmly.

"Are you positive? It's not easy," he responded gently, yet factually.

"I'm positive," I said, as I explained to Clio again what was happening, then leaned over, thanked her, and kissed her goodbye.

Clio passed on in a very peaceful and easy manner. I was actually surprised how beautiful it was, and felt grateful to have spent her last exhale together. She literally exhaled right into my inhale, which is something I will cherish forever. Sharing those last moments with a being is lovelier than I ever imagined, and easier than I ever dreamed. I used to be afraid of death but the animals have taught me how beautiful, magical and special it can be.

Gathering my grey and white blanket, I headed back to my car solemnly—this time without my dear Clio. Mara met me at the driver's side with a huge hug, then walked back around and got in. I thanked her profusely for being there for us, and for making me laugh during a really challenging time.

Mara headed back to her home, while I returned to an entirely different energy in mine. With only Java remaining, wiggling frantically in her crate, the energy buzzed with exciting adventure. Our space was now filled with one feisty dog whose spirit was as big as the world, and one feisty woman whose spirit was ready to soar.

Clipping a green, braided leash to her whimsically dancing body, Java and I hopped in my SUV, and grieved Clio's death over a single, vanilla ice cream cone.

CHAPTER EIGHT

RESPECT

"R-E-S-P-E-C-T.

Find out what it means to me."

~ Aretha Franklin

Aretha Franklin is really something, but Etta James rocks my world. An oversized, brassy, brazen goddess, she can rip up the house with her sexual antics and soulful sound. I've seen, heard, and touched Miss Etta James. She's a rock-solid woman who exemplifies all that it means to love yourself completely no matter what shape, size, or color you are.

Long before I finished her biography, *Rage to Survive,* I knew she was a key player in my life because I shared a silent kinship with her. I'm sure you've idolized people before, but have you ever felt like you've met an angel at the House of Blues? In her lifetime, Etta's seen some crazy, nasty stuff. Somehow, she managed to forgive those who had hurt her, and learned to love herself again after she was lost to heroin.

While I've never been lost to heroin, I have felt lost before. After my Dad and Clio died in the same week, I felt *really* lost and disconnected. In order to help find myself again, I cranked the music of sweet Etta James, and made it a priority to hug my soul.

If you've ever felt lost, it takes precious time and energy to get back on track and feel grounded again. Usually, it involves letting go and giving it up to the Universe—wiping your hands clean of trying to control the outcomes. Chocolate helps, too.

We can't actually control the outcomes, but if we play our cards right, sometimes the Universe opens up and sends us a free bonus gift. In order to receive the gift, we need to pay attention. Magic usually appears when we need it the most, and it almost always appears by surprise. That's why it's called magic.

With my thirty fifth birthday just around the corner, Etta James 'magically' scheduled a live show in my hometown of Madison, Wisconsin on the exact date of my birthday, June 28. Many years ago, a psychic in New Orleans told me I was going to have a life changing experience when I was thirty-five. At the time, I was in my late twenties, so thirty-five seemed a long way off. As it got closer, I pulled out that bit of information and wondered what would happen.

Etta James was willing to meet me halfway to creating a life changing experience, and it was my job to meet her halfway. As difficult as it can be to ask for what you want, it's also incredible to see what happens when you actually *do* ask. What I wanted more than anything, was to share Etta James with my friends. All I needed to do was ask.

Sending out invitations, I informed my friends that I would gladly pay $20 of each Etta James ticket they bought, thinking this would be an incentive for them to join me. To my surprise, twenty friends bought tickets to the show, and none of them were willing to take me up on my offer to help pay for their tickets. My friends knew what a big deal this was, and they were eager to fill up the first few rows at the concert to help celebrate a new year in my life.

Arriving early at the Barrymore Theater in Madison, I made a beeline to try to get backstage to talk with Etta's son, Donto. He was also the band's drummer and he was my 'in' with Etta. Donto and I first met at one of his Mom's shows in San Francisco years back.

He and I sat in the lobby and talked about the recording industry during intermission, and at that time in my life, I was performing with a steel drum band. Donto was running a recording studio, so we chatted about the difficulties of recording steel drums, and I promised him I'd mail him a copy of one of our CDs. The steel band was a mixture of hot Caribbean sounds and Jimmy Buffett, and it's funny now to gloss over ten years of my life as a rock star, but it really has nothing to do with dogs or women.

Having performed at the same venue myself, I knew the ins and outs of the Barrymore Theater. Walking to the loading dock behind the building, I carried a large white envelope with me that contained a handwritten thank you note for Etta James. Attached to the note was a photo of us together that was taken at a show in New Orleans a year earlier. Also included in the envelope was another copy of one of my band's CDs for Donto, in case he never received the first one I'd sent. At worst case, I would be rejected. At best case, I would be accepted.

As I nearly skipped toward the loading dock with excitement, a guy bigger than a triple-decker sandwich came to greet me. Smiling confidently, I quickly flashed the picture of Etta and I in hopes that it would soften my entrance. And just in case that didn't work, I was smiling the kindest, most honest smile I have. The guy looked right past me and my big smile, then pointed directly at the photo of Etta and I.

"How in the world did you get that? Etta don't take her picture with anyone!" he asked in amazement.

"I just asked her," I responded.

I went on to explain the creative story of how I asked the usher at a show in New Orleans if I could talk with Etta and get a photo. All I wanted to do was thank her for making such a difference in my life, so all I did was ask if I could. I'm not sure anyone had ever really asked something like that before because the usher beckoned a fancily dressed woman in a silk mustard suit to try to figure me out. I was honest and respectful, and she let me backstage. I continued to tell him the hilarious story of how I literally chased Etta down the hallway—talking at high speed while she raced at higher speeds on her cherry-red scooter.

"Excuse me, Etta? Could I please have a photo with you?" I asked quickly while my friend Carrie ran backwards with three cameras to snap a photo.

"Do I have to stop?" Etta bounced back.

"Well, not if you don't want to," I beamed and laughed as she screeched to a halt then turned to me and smiled.

Resting my arm around her broad shoulders, Etta and I both smiled for the camera.

Click.

"I've listened to your music for years and wanted to thank you for making such a huge difference in my life. I traveled from Wisconsin to see your show tonight and hopefully get a chance to thank you in person," I blurted out at lightning speed. I could hear Etta's mind rattling with poignant questions.

Why on earth would a tall, skinny white girl from Wisconsin travel all the way to New Orleans just to see me?

Girl, are you nuts?

Etta paused, shifted her thinly painted eyebrows in curiosity, then peered over at me out of the side of her expressive eyes.

"Really?" she questioned in amazement.
As the big, bouncer and I laughed at my story of how I met Etta James, Donto came around the corner. I could feel him

looking at me and wondering why this tall, skinny, white girl was hanging out with this huge, black, bouncer and laughing over pictures and stories of his mother.

"Hi, I'm Sage. We met in San Francisco a few years ago and talked about recording steel drums. I sent you my CD but never knew if you got it. I brought another one..."

"I remember you!" With excitement in his voice, Donto continued, "My Mom stole the CD you sent me and wouldn't stop playing it. I'm so glad you brought me another one."

Etta James was listening to *my* music all the while I was listening to hers. Okay, that's magic.

Handing the envelope directly to Donto, I asked if he'd please give it to his Mom. Then, I asked a personal favor — that if it was possible, I'd love to hear Etta sing *Out of the Rain*.

"Well, I'll see what I can do. I'm not sure any of us even know that one, except mom," Donto laughed, as he took the envelope from my hand.

Donto and I chatted a little while longer about rock and roll stuff, then I told him I was attending the show with twenty friends to celebrate my thirty fifth birthday.

"It was really nice of your Mom to play here for my birthday," I joked with him. He smiled back, wished me a Happy Birthday, and we parted.

Catching up with my friends, my backstage escapades became prime dinner conversation. I was on fire with excitement, and eager to experience Etta James with my friends. When the show was about to start, we all headed inside to secure our seats in the second and third row—a bit disappointed there was no room for dancing.

How can I possibly sit in a chair and just <u>listen</u> to Etta James without dancing?

Looking around, I noticed other people in the audience who looked familiar, as the sound man came up to wish me a Happy Birthday. Then one of the ushers wished me the same. Without Etta even on stage yet, my birthday was more than I could ever have dreamed of.

How did they know it was my birthday?

Then Miss Etta James took the stage and raised the bar. For nearly two and a half hours, and no break, Etta brought down the house with her more than usual array of sexual antics. She was in rare form that night and I wondered if she'd sing the song I'd requested on the thank you letter I'd handed to the bouncer before the show.

Surrounded by people I loved who also loved me, I looked around to see smiles and joy from my friends and family— most of them sharing the Etta James experience for their first time. As the first notes of *At Last* floated sweetly from Etta's lips, I moved back a row to sit next to my Mom and hold her hand. Emotion flowed from my eyes and heart as Etta sang her signature song.

The warmth of my Mom's hand in mine made me smile, as I turned to her and whispered,

"Dad saw Etta sing this same song in 1961 in New Orleans." Wiping tears of gratitude from my eyes, I said softly, "I miss him, Mom."

"I miss him too, honey," she replied gently, then squeezed my warm hand in hers. Sitting hand in hand, my Mom and I finished out the song together, then I got up to head back to my seat.

"Thank you for being here. I love you, Mom."

"I love you a bunch, honey," she replied sweetly.

Etta belted out a few more raucous blues tunes, then thanked the band and the audience. I was a bit disappointed that the show was coming to a close, but grateful for the amazing show she had given us. What I didn't realize was that Etta wasn't done yet. She had a special birthday gift for me.

Funky bass and drum rhythms merged with a full horn section as Etta opened her mouth, and my jaw dropped three stories. Like smoke wafting gracefully from a smoldering fire, Etta linked Al Green's *Love and Happiness* with a soulful, sexy rendition of *Happy Birthday*, directly to me!

I sat in complete disbelief next to my Grand Canyon pal, Ellen, and heard my name come out of Etta James' mouth repeatedly. There couldn't have been a better gift than that, as I listened in awe while the audience hoot-hoot-hooted for Etta to continue her signature, erotic chair dance.

"Go up there!!!" Ellen rattled me out of my love trance, and pointed to the stage which was only eight feet away.

Getting up as if in a dream, I walked four short steps down the aisle and in front of the stage I went—to watch my idol sing *Happy Birthday* to me. Etta watched me get closer as our eyes connected deeply. Resting my hand over my heart, I mouthed 'Thank you' to her amidst a huge smile. Smiling back, Etta touched her own heart with her left hand, then blew a kiss to me which continues to rest sweetly in my soul to this day.

Now, that's some real birthday magic!

I wonder what would have happened if I had forced my way into getting a picture with Etta in New Orleans instead of asking. If I'd been demanding, instead of respectful, I'm guessing she would have remembered me in a very different light, and I doubt she'd sing to me on my birthday. She must have read my thank you note before the show.

My parents taught me to have manners and write thank you notes when someone did something nice. I just thought it was common sense to write Etta a thank you note for being such a key player in my life. Respect goes a long way.

Humility, honor and respect are values I work hard to manifest in my life on a daily basis. I continue to learn the most about respect from working with the animals in my life. We can move closer to a person or animal freely, but if they're not ready to receive we can scare them away easily and quickly. It takes very little to be respectful of others. All it entails is thinking about *them* instead of only you. Respect involves an immense amount of unconditional love—to be able to give without receiving or curtail your giving until the receiver is ready. When they're ready to receive, it's incredible for both parties.

By having Java show up in my life, I was given the opportunity to improve my level of respect for all beings. Sometimes respect meant holding still, and allowing Java to come to me. From holding still, without desire or judgment, I learned how lovely it is when an animal feels enough trust and respect to take those few steps toward you. When you give them the respect they deserve, they'll often lick you on the nose with a thank you note. Over and over, Java taught me how to touch, where to touch, and when to touch. When I overstepped her boundaries, she'd walk away and we'd start all over again.

Imagine if people touched your body whenever *they* felt like it, and however and wherever *they* wanted to. Our saving grace as humans is that we can give verbal feedback and tell someone what feels nice and what doesn't. We can also just walk or run away because we don't have leashes attached to us. When animals are given the choice to move closer, stay still, or move farther away, it all comes down to how respected, loved, and trusted they feel. When they're leashed, they don't always feel that they have a choice.

It took me quite awhile to realize that Java didn't tolerate people who overstepped her boundaries, and that it was me who needed to help her out. When she was on a leash, if someone approached her, she would often lunge and snap. If she was off leash, she was able to make a simpler choice and just move away. Java's a gorgeous dog, so when we go for walks, people stop, stare, and often want to touch her— usually on top of her head, because that's what humans do. She can't tolerate that, so I've learned to help her out by asking the people nicely not to overstep her boundaries. I have also taught Java how to sit at my side and look at me when she comes across something that's challenging for her— a bike, a stranger, another dog.

What if a stranger walked up to you at the grocery store and patted you on the head without asking? Most people would describe that as disrespectful (and weird), yet we do that with animals all the time. It's fascinating to me how much animals will tolerate sometimes, but having a dog who doesn't tolerate everything has taught me more about respect and trust than anything.

When Java came to my art classroom every Friday, I taught the kids how to respect Java by touching her chest or shoulder first rather than the top of her head. Kids always want to know *why*, so I explained to them that it didn't feel nice to her to have her head touched—that it scared her and that she doesn't always make smart choices when she's scared. Then I *showed* them why by having them put their own hand in front of their face. They were surprised to find that their breathing stopped and they too felt uncomfortable and scared. When they placed their hand on their chest, they exhaled, smiled and understood.

It can be difficult to set boundaries, but when you have a challenging dog, you learn that it's necessary in order to keep everyone safe. My job is to help keep Java safe and to help her make good choices. Part of that means teaching humans the best way to approach (or not approach) her. Java makes great choices when people squat down and let her come to them, but if they lean over and reach for her, it's too much, too fast and she reacts quickly. I used to want her to be friendly to everyone she ever met, but I realized that we're not there yet. We may never be, and that's okay, too. Sometimes, we expect way too much from our animals. I know I have.

The challenge for us as humans is to find a respectful way to touch animals, and each other, in order to build self-esteem, confidence, and improve body awareness without taking away anything in return. If we move closer to those we love, and they're not ready for that much closeness, we may find they continue to move further away. If we touch in ways that don't feel nice to the receiver, the receiver moves even further away.

The magic of respect lies in having the desire in your heart to help another being to feel comfortable and safe on this planet. And when you find the magic, I guarantee you'll receive some sort of thank you note.

CHAPTER NINE

TRUST

"Sometimes you just have to leap,

and build your wings on the way down."

~ Kobi Yamada

Everything happens for a reason. With my Dad and Clio gone, I began to open my heart like I never knew possible. Grieving can be a lonely process. It can completely consume you if you let it, or it can completely free you. I was lucky enough to have talked with my Dad about death long before it happened—to find out how he truly felt about his mortality and what his wishes were. Many years ago, we shared a beautiful conversation, which took place on his boat near Isla Tortuga (Turtle Island) in Costa Rica, and somehow I felt okay about his death. I still miss him like crazy, but having peace with a being before they pass is a blessed experience. With Clio, I grieved a ton with her before she passed on. Now it was Java's turn to grieve.

Clio hadn't been gone very long, and I was surprised how lonely the house felt without her—and how much larger Java's spirit seemed to become. But no matter how much I tried to explain beforehand that Clio was leaving us, it broke my heart to watch Java continue to look for her weeks afterward. She became more anxious, attached to my pant leg, and afraid to go outside alone. This lasted for what seemed like months, and I began to read books about the grieving process with animals. We were obviously grieving together. Java began to pull harder on a leash, and started to snarl more at other dogs and people. With Clio's passing, Java shifted into becoming a more nervous dog, and I went back to desensitizing her to everything I'd already done as a puppy—bikes, men, skateboards, mops—you name it.

My second TTouch Training was only a few weeks away and I was eager to learn more to help us both understand and grow. With school out for the summer, I began my case studies for my TTouch certification by working with dogs from the same shelter where I picked up Java only a year and a half before. Twice a week for two months I worked with two dogs, Austin and Teenie. Both dogs displayed a lack of confidence that manifested in completely opposite ways. Teenie stayed a great distance away, while Austin charged closer, then used his strong mouth to defend.

By using what I had learned, I was able to help Austin and Teenie make better choices, and feel better about themselves in a short while. Both dogs required the same thing—respect, love and understanding. By using the TTouch Half Body Wrap, a variety of TTouches and the Confidence Course, Austin and Teenie's issues lessened dramatically and both dogs were finally on their way to new homes.

I immersed myself in my animal work during the summer— finally reading the green TTouch book that plopped off my shelf a few months back, and working with any animal who presented itself. I felt at home with animals and kids, yet I knew I wouldn't last more than two additional years as an art teacher in the public schools. Somehow, I wanted to work the two in together.

If I can do this with animals, why can't I do the same with kids?

At the end of July, Java and I left for our second TTouch Training—this time, a thirteen-hour drive to Cincinnati, Ohio. Only three months earlier I had been scared to death to travel four hours with this hound, and now I was excited for an entire day alone with her on the road. I learned quickly to discern how a slight nose nudge on my shoulder meant she needed to go potty, and a couple of persistent nudges meant I'd better pull the car over quickly. She learned that Taco Bell® has *great* seven-layer burritos and that pay tolls are absolutely fascinating. We stayed at the Econo Lodge® together for a week during the training, and this time, Java learned how to adjust to all of the nuances. There was no lunging at the mirrors, and very little barking at odd noises that bumped in the night. Me, I learned how to trust and breathe.

Session Two was taught by Jodi Frediani. Jodi was a bubbly, vibrant instructor from California who sported wild, curly, dark hair, and a great spiritual sense. It was during my second training where I began to take a good look at myself instead of focusing completely on Java. I began to relax, let go and breathe, and learned to trust both in TTouch and my own choices. As an added bonus lesson, I also learned that Java was a wonderful dog with a few issues that could actually be helped with the right resources.

Journal Entry
7/23/02 - TTouch Training: Session 2, Day 1

Great TTouch intro this morning. Java walked up to complete strangers at break time, then laid down and chewed a bone during class. She gave a slight growl when she noticed a dog across the room, but calmed a lot in the first half hour. I'm amazed at the difference since the last training. She was asleep in her crate before lunch—went in on her own. She gets really agitated when she needs sleep. So do I. Big moan in her crate, stretching, calming signals (yawn/licks)—all before lunch. After lunch she was calmer with me sitting next to her. She was tired and hot but doing really well. Less reacting to barking!

Journal Entry
7/25/02 -TTouch Training: Session 2, Day 3

Java was asleep all morning until break! She did great with people and dogs moving about, and fell sound asleep after break with her body outstretched and relaxed. She's starting to face the circle of people and dogs more and uses calming signals on her own. I'm so pleased!

I continued to watch in awe as other people worked with Java in the Confidence Course, and I saw how much potential she exuded. My TTouch colleagues fell in love with her as they understood better, and because Java worked so diligently and taught so well. Within very little time, my quiet friend Kelly began to open up. She and I hung out more and more together, and during Session Two we became inseparable.

On shelter visit days we were often found skidding behind the wildest dogs with the longest list of issues—both laughing hysterically and loving it all the while. Somehow, Kelly and I were able to settle these dogs quickly with TTouches, Body Wraps and work in the Confidence Course or Playground for Higher Learning, and together we helped them become more focused and confident.

Strangely enough, Kelly and I both began to trust *ourselves*, and build our own confidence and self-esteem through Tellington TTouch®.

As the week progressed, Java became more confident, and I became more aware of how much confidence I still lacked. It's tough when your dog points out your shortcomings, but it's also an exercise in gratitude.

Journal Entry
7/28/02 - TTouch Training: Session 2, Day 6

HUGE SUCCESS!! When I returned from dinner, I took Java to the outside pen to run. Three dogs were running on the other side of the fence. A large, black shepherd ran up to the fence, greeted Java, then barked at her. Both Java and the other dog ran away from each other, and then a Rottweiler and another mixed breed ran to the fence to greet Java as well. Java lifted her hackles and put her head and tail down while the Rottie was sniffing her through the fence.

She averted her gaze, then wagged her tail and went into a play bow. She ran up to the dogs, wagged, barked, and then bounced back to me—nosing my leg and running back to the fence to say hello again. I gave her a lot of praise and it was an absolute delight to see her wag her tail around dogs. I could tell she was really proud of herself, too!

Java was learning to stand on her own four feet and make appropriate choices for herself. Watching the pride in her eyes and her body as she made a wise choice was enough to fluff my heart three sizes. Java would often glance at me sideways as if to say, "Did you see that? Did you see that? I did it!" And the more confident she became, the more I was able to use my energy to look inward.

It's hard to look inward. We often find excuses not to do so because it requires that we sit still and take an inventory of who we really are, or who we want to become. It's much easier to point the finger outwards, but the finger will eventually come back and point at our self. There were many moments during my second training where I felt like a failure—that it was my fault Java was so challenging.

What if I had only done this, that, or the other thing?

During the last day of the training, it hit me. Java trusted me more than I trusted her and I needed to let go and have faith. She looked to *me* to make decisions, and it was my own insecurity that still made me flounder.

As the final day of the training came to a close, we gathered in our circle to share what we learned over the week. This time I was determined to overcome my fear and speak up before Java made me do it. I took a deep breath and knew I was going to cry before my mouth even opened. Looking around the circle at these eighteen people and twelve animals who were now family, I thanked each of them profusely. I felt like we were on a speed course to enlightenment.

"My week was incredible," I began confidently, "It was really difficult, but I learned a lot about myself. I learned that this sweet, little girl by my side trusts me a lot more than I trust her."

The tears came pouring out as Java leaned her head on my leg and looked up at me—reflecting moral support through the white crescent moons on the bottom of her deep, brown eyes.

"I also realized I need to let go, trust and have enough faith that she's going to be alright—to allow Java the freedom to grow and change," I finished, then stroked the side of Java's muzzle.

My words were short and sweet but the lesson was grandiose. I looked up to see my colleagues smiling back with tears streaming down their faces, as I wiped my own tears from my eyes. We were all making a difference in ourselves, and in the animals.

Partway through the closing ceremony, we took a quick potty break. Jodi, the instructor, had gently laid out a circle of Jamie Sams' *Medicine Cards* (St. Martin's Press, New York) to help provide spiritual guidance for the group. As Java and I got up for the break, she again made a beeline for the center of the circle.

Java stood tall and proud, stretched, looked around to make sure everyone was watching, then *STOMPED* her big, brown paw down onto one of the cards. Jodi and I looked at each other with eyes and mouths popped wide open.

143

"Don't you want to know which card she picked!?" Jodi squealed in amazement.

Of course I did! Walking over to the only card with Plott Hound claw marks on it, I picked it up and noticed an image of a porcupine on the opposing side. Porcupine meant absolutely nothing to me until I read the description aloud in the accompanying *Medicine Card* book.

"Porcupine, remind me of innocence again — with every man a brother, each woman a friend." I went on to read, "The south of the medicine wheel is the place of childlike innocence and humility. It is the home of playfulness, and the position of Porcupine on the medicine wheel of life."

What came next sent shivers up and down everyone's spine as I continued on, "Porcupine has many special qualities, and a very powerful medicine; the power of faith and trust."

Ten minutes earlier those same words fell out of my mouth, and now I wondered who was steering the ship — Java, me, the Universe, or all of us. A huge lump formed in my throat as I swallowed deeply, then looked over cautiously at Jodi with the whites of *my* eyes showing. In that very moment, I knew my connection with Java ran deeper than I could possibly comprehend Java and I gave hugs, then said our thank yous and goodbyes. Kelly and I made it a point to stay better connected before our next TTouch Training, and then Java's Aunt Judy and Aunt Kathy waited for one last lick on the nose from Java.

Java and I drove home completely exhausted and more connected than ever before. Even a small glance started to make sense, and we understood each other better in every moment. I watched, learned and became aware, as Java learned to do the same. Java and I intended to manifest the faith and trust of porcupine energy, so we had our work cut out for us. First of all, I needed to face my humility and insecurity, and learn to believe in myself more than anything. With the rest of the summer ahead of us, we learned how to trust in each other, and in ourselves, by letting go in tiny bits. I learned to breathe better, and tried to keep a loose leash when we walked, and Java learned that it was possible for humans to let go, trust and have faith. She was *very* patient with me while I was continuing to learn more patience.

Even though starting an animal business seemed light years away, I was anxious to include porcupine medicine into a business name. Lying in bed together one morning, I looked over at Java,

"What should we name our business, Girlie?" I smiled playfully at her.

Java looked back at me with soft eyes, then cocked her head as if to say. "Hmmm. I don't know. Let's brainstorm!"

Grabbing a pen and piece of paper from my night stand, I began writing down every quality I saw in Java when she was feeling good about herself, and every lesson I learned through my first four months of TTouch Training. The words flowed quickly from my heart onto the paper as my page became covered with black ink. Stopping for a brief moment to catch my breath and reconnect with Java, I looked over to see she was still looking back at me.

"I really love you, girl," I smiled deeply, as I placed my hand on her chest. Then, Java leaned forward and licked me on the nose. I could tell she loved me, too.

My page was filled with words of love, understanding, trust, faith, balance, coordination, respect, awareness, and confidence. I continued to wonder how any of those words coincided with a porcupine, but it took only moments for me to figure it out. Java was misunderstood. Porcupines are misunderstood. If their quills are down, they're very docile animals. Java is docile if she's feeling good about herself. But if porcupine quills are up, they remind me of Java snarling at the end of her leash.

What if a porcupine was dancing?

Would anyone be afraid of it?

Would people understand that a porcupine is only a porcupine until we add a judgment to it?

While Java and I sat in bed and brainstormed together, my animal training business, Dancing Porcupine, was born (www.DancingPorcupine.com). I was one step closer to my dream of making money petting animals. With a background as a graphic designer, I was eager to design a logo, and get the identity for Dancing Porcupine started. By the end of the summer, I had a fabulous business name with a delightful story behind it, and a whimsical logo to match. Now all I needed was to create the life I wanted, and what I desired most was to share my life with another being.

Once you write something down, the Universe takes it into serious consideration. I was very connected to spirit and often read about shamanism, animals, or something from the other side. I was a spiritual sponge, and spent a lot of time and energy praying, meditating, and trusting. I felt a strong desire growing inside my heart, and I felt ready to move forward. So, by the light of the full September moon, I laid in bed and prayed. As the moonlight danced across my silhouette, I prayed for a man to come to me—one who would love me as much as I loved him. Then I added a second prayer that maybe, *just maybe*, he would love animals as much as I did.

That night, I went to sleep with a huge smile on my face, and an even bigger sigh of relief in my heart. It was out of my hands now. The rest was up to the Universe.

Trust. Faith. Letting Go.

CHAPTER TEN

CHANGE

"Change is inevitable.

Growth is optional."

~ Walt Disney

Allen showed up in my life one month later. Ready or not, there he was. The date was October 5, 2002, and I woke to find a fifteen-foot tree branch that had crashed to the ground in my front yard. Dropping with it was a two-foot long wishbone-shaped twig I had deemed a symbol of partnership almost two years earlier.

Many days I laid on my couch in peaceful meditation, watching this loose twig rock back and forth like a pendulum—wondering how it balanced so gracefully through sleet, wind, rain and snow without ever falling.

With the two wishbone parts pointing to the earth, and one single twig pointing to the sky, this determined little twig rocked itself to sleep day after day. It signified the strength, balance, and mutual love I desired in a true spiritual partnership. Although the strong support branch had crashed to the earth below, the fragile, little wishbone branch lay unharmed. I paid attention.

Walking outside with fresh tree limb energy vibrating around me, I reached down, picked up the little branch, and took it inside to rest on my bookshelf. It was a Saturday morning and I was headed to a two-day workshop to learn and practice shamanic journeying. I felt like I was going to meet someone special.

Since the man of my dreams was surely going to magically appear before my eyes at the workshop, I wanted to make sure I chose my clothes carefully. Putting on my favorite patched up Levi's® and a dark red t-shirt with a bright, orange, vortex pattern in the center, I checked how my butt looked in my pants, fixed my hair, then kissed Java goodbye. With my Ashiko drum under my arm, I set out for the day's adventure—spiritual guidance with a mutual love chaser.

Driving to downtown Madison, I felt incredibly alive inside. The fallen branch made me think about the past, wonder about the future, and express gratitude for how beautifully the pieces of my life were fitting together in that moment. In order to pay for the workshop in the first place, I sold handmade candles at a Wisconsin Greyhound Pets of America event a month earlier. The only reason I started making candles in the first place was because I didn't have a lot of money for Christmas gifts the year after my divorce.

So, with most of the events in my life fitting together so precisely and neatly, I have little doubt about the power of the Universe, and my own connection to spirit. I've heard others say that there are no accidents. I believe. I felt strong and ready to embark on my own shamanic journeys after having spent time doing shamanic work with Ana in the past. I was in a place in my spiritual growth of wanting to find ways to get the guidance I needed, yet I was searching for a method that spoke to me. Animals, nature and drumming. That spoke to me.

We all have the opportunity to choose the best method of spiritual guidance for ourselves. However, we often choose the easiest route or the route that is the most acceptable by society. None of my friends or family knew anything about shamanic work, and here I was, spending two days immersed in something that felt right to me and unclear to others. It's a freeing feeling to do what feels right to *you* instead of what feels right to everyone else.

As I parked my car at the workshop, I grabbed my drum from the back seat. Then, I looked around to see if anyone else looked like workshop-type people. Me being me, I headed toward the closest building I saw, and pretended I knew what I was doing. Uncertainty can be masked as confidence when you don't mind being wrong, but after checking the address on the building, I felt fairly confident that I was right. A mismatched couple walked up behind me and asked if I knew where the shamanic workshop was being held.

"Up here, I think," I responded quickly.

Without truly noticing them, I led the way as the three of us headed up the stairs together. I followed the noise coming from the end of the hall, took off my shoes at the door and entered. I immediately scanned the room for the man of my dreams, then noticed a beautiful woman taking registration forms at the door. Long, dark, braided hair fell neatly down her back, and as she turned to take my form, I smiled. It was Ana. I hadn't seen her in months, and it felt nice to reconnect with her since our private shamanic work together. A huge hug and a smile, she glistened with a mirror of radiant energy.

"I'm *so* glad to see you here. This is going to be an amazing two days for you," Ana said, as she marked my name off on the registration.

Ana and I talked for a few minutes, then I browsed the faces in the room to find the perfect place to plant myself among the circle of people. Spotting a kind looking woman with long, flowing, grey hair, I walked across the circle in her direction. The woodsy smell of cedar and sage smoke filled the air with density and life.

"Is this spot taken?" I asked with a smile.

"Nope," she replied, then she scooted over and smiled kindly back at me.

She seemed very genuine, and for some reason she looked a bit familiar. Situating my blanket on the floor, I laid out the requested objects I had brought along to help with my journeying experience—an orange bandana to block the light during my journeys, a rock from Costa Rica to help with guidance, and a journal to record my findings.

Once I settled into my space, I was onto bigger and better things. Like a snake flitting its tongue out to sense what's in her path, I scanned the room again to see which guy I was supposed to meet.

Nope, not him.
Not him either.
Hmmm. No thank you.

After scanning impatiently, I started to wonder if the fallen wishbone twig meant anything at all, or if I was just playing some sort of game in my mind. As I continued to send my gaze around the room, my eyes locked deeply with a man who had shown his face to me in a dream three months earlier. In my dream, this man's exact face appeared, and he was wearing a white-on-white embroidered linen outfit of baggy pants, and a matching peasant shirt. To see him in reality before me was both comforting and surreal. A cleancut, nearly bald man with a perfect, blonde mustache, he had the kindest, gentlest, sea green eyes I'd ever seen. We exchanged brief smiles, then waved a quick hello as I noticed a sparkle light up my heart. Shivers danced up and down my spine, then I looked away to compose myself.

When you meet someone special, you know they're special right away. There's an energetic lifeline that connects you immediately with them. Moments like this don't happen very often in a lifetime, but when they do, they strike passionately. Deep soul connections are an incredible gift to behold.

As I fumbled with my rock and bandana (pretending I was doing something important), I watched this gentle man who was sitting two spots away, on the other side of the woman with the long, grey hair. I couldn't figure it out. I was really confused because the connection was strong for me when I looked at him, yet it seemed like he and the goddess-like woman were together. I mean, *together*.

My head crinkled up with wonder, while my heart and soul opened with desire. A huge rush of energy flowed through my body as the excitement of possibility rose. Maybe he *was* the one. Looking more closely, the man looked to be about twenty years younger than her, yet they held matching drums and sat on matching mats. It wasn't clear to me if he was available or not.

Maybe I was wrong.
Maybe they really are a couple.

By now, I was almost staring at the two of them. The goddess-like woman looked over and smiled, and I quickly figured out why she looked so familiar to me. This seemingly mismatched couple was the inquisitive man and woman who followed me up the stairs at the start of the workshop, and I hadn't really looked at either one of them to the point of truly *seeing* until I sat down. The first exercise for the workshop was to journey with a partner to gain guidance for them.

The activity involved one person posing a question, and the other connecting with their animal or spirit guides through a sort of trance-like state called shamanic journeying. The purpose of the exercise was to learn how to be open to guidance from spirit for not only yourself, but others as well. Thinking about what sort of questions I had, my heart settled on one specific one.

"How will I know when I'm ready to be in an intimate relationship?" I asked impatiently.

"The time is now," she replied softly, then smiled confidently.

She laid her body next to mine—our legs and arms touching—and the steady, heartbeat drumming began. I felt myself sort of wondering what she might find, then relaxing into a dark, gentle abyss. My mind floated into a place of nothingness as my breathing became shallow and slow. While she was journeying for me, my task was to be open to receiving. When the journey came to an end, five rhythmic drum beats brought us both back to reality, and she quickly reported her findings.

"I saw a bonfire," she said slowly, as I waited eagerly for her next morsel of information. "Eskimo people were sitting in a circle and passing bowls of food to the right. A woman with long, blonde hair appeared on a horse but the horse careened off a cliff. You came crawling up the side of the cliff with an incredible amount of determination. *You* were the woman on the horse."

Smiling and nodding vigorously I began to make associations with the images she saw—how they fit with my life and desires—my strength, determination, and burning desire to go after what I want.

She continued, "You were bathed in white light and almost levitated across the ravine. A group of blackbirds carried pink ribbons in their beaks and tied them all over your body like a Maypole. Trust your intuition," she ended gracefully as she patted me gently on the leg. I thanked her, then recorded her words in my journal.

Next, we gathered in small groups, and I filled the only empty spot in the circle—between the goddess-like woman, and this gentle guy who appeared to be her partner, friend, or both. We shared our journeys among the group, and I found my heart wandering to the man on my left. Looking over, I saw the most stunning silver ring on his right hand. Perched solidly on his ring finger was a huge silver eagle head that possessed the energy of a live eagle soaring strongly above the water, yet gentle as a summer breeze. I reached over and touched his ring, noticed how beautiful and strong his hands were, and stumbled for my words.

"Wow! That's a *really* cool ring!"

Good one, Sage.

His eyes smiled back at mine and that was all it took for me to wonder about him even more. His smile was the most genuine and loving I'd ever laid eyes on and it pierced my heart, in a good way. I could feel the strength of his energy, and the kindness in his heart, and it felt incredible.

"I'm Allen," he smiled back to me, as his eyes met mine again.

"Hi…*(long pause)*….I'm Sage."

How is it that some women can float into a room and get noticed and others stammer over everything, and also get noticed?

Lucille Ball *is* my soul sister, so calamity comes naturally. I felt kind of clumsy around him, yet I wanted to get to know him better. How I was going to make that happen, I was clueless, but then an invitation for lunch answered my question.

Gladly accepting, Allen, the goddess woman, and I headed to a bistro a block away to enjoy some sunshine and conversation. Ordering a veggie sandwich and a bowl of soup, I noticed Allen order something similar. Grabbing my tray, I seated myself at the only empty place at the table which was next to Allen. With a warm fall breeze tickling the October sunshine, Allen and I easily engaged in deep conversation about photographic memory, the mind, and how to rescue the poor little bee who fell into his bowl of hot, vegetable soup. Here was a guy who loved animals as much as I did, and was also a vegetarian. On the way back from lunch, I found myself looking at his strong shoulders and chest underneath his long sleeve, yellow shirt, then wondering what his butt *really* looked like under those tan, baggy dress pants.

Finally, Allen and I were paired up together for a drumming activity in the afternoon. The idea was that one person would drum a word, thought, or feeling, and the other person would hopefully receive it. In layman terms, this means that one person drums while focusing their thoughts on an image, and the other person tries to connect with the other person's thoughts and receive their image.

Grabbing my drum, I began a slow heartbeat rhythm. Then, I thought really hard about my favorite tree, the willow. I let my mind visualize an entire grove of willow trees dancing in the breeze—waving their long, lean branches slowly, yet confidently—while the rhythm of their dance pounded on the drum. Back and forth, back and forth, cha, cha, cha. I concentrated harder than I think I've ever concentrated before because I really wanted it to work.

Maybe this guy can read my mind!
I wonder if he thinks I'm hot. He's got great hands!
Willow tree, willow tree, willow tree.

After ten minutes of filling my head with willow trees, and more willow trees, I stopped and peeked over at Allen. He smiled and I almost fainted from giddiness.

"I got waves," he said in his soft, gentle voice, and then cocked his head much like Java to see if we'd properly achieved the mind meld.

"I was drumming an image of a willow tree," I smiled back, feeling a little disappointed.

Allen's entire body lit up as he vibrantly exclaimed, "I *love* willow trees!! They're my favorite!!"

I thought to myself that I've never seen anyone get this excited about willow trees, smiled back shyly, and said, "Mine, too."

Then, we switched roles. Allen drummed and I worked my butt off to try to get the images he was sending. All that kept coming to me was the word love.

Love.
Love.
LOVE!
Am I making this up?
Love.

For ten minutes I felt love, love, and more love, and when he finished drumming, I felt somewhat relieved and a little apprehensive to share what I'd received.

"I sent you an image of a horse running across a wide-open field. What did you get?!" Allen eagerly awaited my reply like a five-year-old standing on their tippy toes at the ice cream counter.

"Ummm...*(long pause)* Love," I said sheepishly.

We both smiled shyly, and I felt an even deeper connection between us. When you meet a person who clicks with you on a soul level, moving closer isn't something that's conscious. It just happens.

The group finished out the afternoon in a circle, and as we said goodbye for the day, we headed our separate directions for the night. I drove home with visions of the day still reeling in my mind, body, and soul, wondering what tomorrow might bring. I reminded myself to have patience.

Java greeted me with her usual excitement when I got home, and we laughed and played in the back yard for what seemed like hours. With the sun going down, I lit five tea light candles on my bookshelf, and watched the shadow from the wishbone branch stretch across my ceiling. Java and I snuggled up in the yellow, puffy chair together, and I drifted into a quiet place to process my day. Watching the shadows flicker and flutter, the ring of the telephone startled me from my solace. As I went to pick it up, my intuition told me something was wrong.

It was my principal, Ann, calling to tell me that one of our custodians had just taken his own life. I was heartbroken and shocked. Rick was a guy who showed up in my art room every day after school for years to empty my trash and engage in some sort of simple and easy conversation. He was the kind of guy most people were afraid of because they never took the time to get to know him. A misunderstood guy. A porcupine. I guess I didn't truly know him or maybe I would have seen this coming. For years, I watched Rick go from hiding his face behind his long, stringy, grey hair, to a clean-cut man who seemed to have his life more under control.

I waved to him every day on my way home while he had a smoke in his dark blue, hooded sweatshirt—just barely outside the school grounds in order to play by the rules.

"I just talked to him two days ago in the hall. Something didn't seem right when I asked him how he was. He seemed different," I told Ann.

We talked for quite awhile, trying to figure out what we could have done, should have done, and what we could do now. Hanging up, I felt the quiet stillness of the night return, as one single candle remained lit. The energy in my house felt slow and thick, as I sat in the chair with Java and prayed for Rick's soul to find its way. It wasn't working. The image I kept receiving was of large shards of glass flying all over the place, and it felt disconcerting. As smoke wafted peacefully from the final fizzle of the last candle, I watched the long shadow of the wishbone branch cast itself strongly from the light of the moon. Crawling in bed with Java by my side, I thought about the workshop the next day, and planned to ask Allen and the goddess-like woman what to do about praying for someone who shot himself. Nice, light lunch conversation.

The second day of the workshop, we journeyed much deeper—individually, with partners, and with the entire group. Many times during the day we switched partners, but somehow, Allen and I were never paired up again. I felt a magnetic pull toward Allen, and wanted to find another way to connect with him. I liked him. Remembering our journey with the drum the day before, I thought about the significance of the horse image he sent me, and the willow tree I sent him.

Flipping through my book *Medicine Way* by Ted Andrews (Llewellyn Publishing, Minnesota) I spotted a possible significance of the horse image. A bit surprised and embarrassed at the meaning, I hoped he had a sense of humor, but I was about to find out.

Walking over to Allen, I smiled mischievously, then asked, "Wow! Did you know that horses signify freedom....and male sexual energy?"

Allen turned beat red, threw his head back in a full belly laugh, then chuckled, "Oh geez. What was *I* thinking?"

We both laughed, smiled, and made it a point to have lunch together again that afternoon.

At break time, Allen came over to ask if he could play my drum, and I of course handed it over. I watched him walk around the room and pat, pat, pat the drum, and then walk into the hallway to pat, pat, pat some more. He seemed to be humble, yet possessed a confidence that I found to be quite sexy. With the sweetest look on his face, Allen came back, handed me my drum and informed me that he didn't actually know how to play a drum like that at all. Sweet and honest, I could tell he was interested in me, too.

During lunch, Allen and I talked about how to pray for someone who committed suicide. He listened intently to my feelings about Rick's passing, and my struggle with trying to find a way to help make peace for his soul.

"We could do a meditation together after the workshop if you're up for it," Allen offered, then turned to his friend, the goddess-like woman, to make sure she was up for it as well. They had a 4-1/2 hour drive back to their respective homes in Minneapolis, but it was obvious Allen was not the least bit concerned about time.

"I'd really like that. Thank you," I responded graciously, taking him up on the offer, and feeling grateful to have formed a new a connection.

The shamanism workshop ended later in the day, and as we headed to our cars, I warned both Allen and his friend about Java before they followed me to my house. Almost apologetically, I told them that Java was a bit skittish, and barked quite fiercely at almost every man who walked through my door. I told them how the best bet for success was to move slowly and ignore her for a little while—no direct eye contact or friendly pats on the head. Little did I know, Java was hiding something up her brown, furry sleeve.
She was preparing to become man's best friend.

Walking in the door with apprehension, I let Java out of her crate as she bounced like a pinball from here, to there, to everywhere. Allen sat quietly on the couch, then looked softly at the floor while Java bounced toward his direction. She wasn't barking, yet. Bounding right past me, Java collided into Allen's peaceful body, then looked straight into his heart with her entire body wagging with joy. What followed next amazed me even more. Within seconds, I looked over to see Allen crouched on the dining room floor, laughing and giggling, as Java kissed his mustached face. I was relieved—and jealous.

Way to go girl. Work it!

Java hadn't experienced an appropriate greeting with *any* man who had walked through my door, yet it happened right away with this one. But this man was different. Java and Allen hit it off right away, and it warmed my heart to watch her so at ease.

Was he the one I prayed would come? Java sure thinks so! After about half an hour of sharing stories, I finally found out that Allen wasn't coupled with this woman. He informed me that they practiced hypnosis work together in Minneapolis, and were just friends. With the truth out in the open, I found myself being drawn like a magnet toward Allen's kindness, gentleness, and openness—and I still wanted to see his butt. I started to gather up some snacks to set out on the counter, while Allen grabbed a can of cashews from the bag of snacks he brought with him.

"Would you like some?" he asked sweetly, as he held up the can to shake a few into my hand.

I wondered how he knew that cashews were my favorite, and how charming I thought it was of him to give me some. Munching on cashews together, we walked from room to room as Allen playfully explored the entire space. Java was right at his heels.

"You sure have a great place. It's really calm and relaxing," Allen said, as he asked about my original artwork which I had hung modestly on the walls.

No one had ever asked about my artwork, and now I found myself eager to explain to this man who was so interested—and unbelievably sexy. After a short while, we settled into our meditation space on the floor in the living room. I had no clue how Java would handle stillness with visitors but I prayed that please, just this once, she could handle it. I sat cross-legged and face-to-face with Allen, and the goddess-like woman sat directly behind me to reflect the energy back.

I closed my eyes and took a big exhale, and felt Allen do the same. His breath felt warm, sweet, and close, and I liked it a lot. Yummy, man energy.

With eyes closed and hearts open, we began our meditation together. Java didn't. Every few seconds, she'd leap in between Allen and I, then sneak a kiss or two from him. I apologized profusely, as I worked to get Java into a 'Down Stay' that lasted more than two seconds. He smiled sweetly, then told me what a great dog she was—how it was completely fine with him if she interrupted him with a smooch.

He likes Java!

Allen led me through a guided meditation that included having Rick's body intact, and his soul being sent above freely. Disjointed images of a cherry pie, fire and three dark, black lines floated through my mind, as I found myself immersed in a deep trance. And then Java would bound through the space again, and plant a sloppy, wet kiss on Allen's face. But the deeper into the meditation we got, the more settled Java became. Finally, she was lying down right next to us.

With eyes still closed, I suddenly felt a huge burst of heat in the center of my chest. My heart felt open and free—like a pure, white lotus flower unfolding in the morning sun. This continued for minutes, and I couldn't for the life of me figure out what was going on. Finally, I couldn't stand it anymore so I peeked. Peering out of one eyeball from beneath my closed lids, I saw Allen's hands facing my heart. He was helping to open my heart with his warm and gentle energy. I felt the calmest I'd felt in a long time, and the most spiritually connected to any man I'd ever met. To make sure we didn't forget about her, Java continued to sneak in a kiss every now and again.

We finished the meditation, then all three of us talked about what we saw and felt. However, I didn't mention to Allen how his hands had danced with my heart—at least not yet. Java circled Allen's feet, and he crouched down to thank her for being so patient with us.

We hurried to wrap things up and say our goodbyes so the two of them could head back to their homes in Minneapolis. After exchanging phone numbers and email addresses, I handed each of them a tiny homemade jar of salsa from tomatoes I'd recently harvested from my garden. Allen was absolutely ecstatic—even more ecstatic than he'd been about the willow trees. It wasn't until a few weeks later that I felt an even deeper kinship with him, as he informed me that salsa is his absolute favorite food group—followed closely by vanilla chocolate-chip ice cream.

Me, too!

Hugging the goddess-like woman first, we set an intention to keep in touch. I thanked her for her warmth, wisdom, and guidance, then I turned to hug Allen. Time slowed to that place of amorous bliss—where love songs write themselves, and images of living happily forever fill your heart. Reaching my right arm up and my left arm down, I found myself fitting perfectly into his well-muscled arms and chest as we hugged goodbye. As I closed my eyes and inhaled, the scent on the right side of his neck made me want him more. I'm sure we only hugged for a millisecond in real time, but it was as if I knew him before in a past life. It felt like home—the kind of hug where you melt into each other's body like two puzzle pieces waiting to find each other and become joined as one.

His friend said goodbye, then walked down the sidewalk to the car, but Allen hung back just long enough for me to know he was definitely interested. I thanked him again for the meditation and deep conversation, then he walked out my front door. Pausing a brief moment, he turned back toward me and smiled. Propping my screen door open with his body, Allen looked straight into my sea green eyes with the mirror of his. Reaching toward me, he gently touched my right arm with his warm, left hand, then sent a sparkle from his heart to mine.

"I'll talk to you soon," he whispered quietly.

Swallowing a gulp of girlish giddiness, I reached out and briefly embraced his strong, left arm in return. This was the man I dreamt would walk into my life, and my heart confirmed it to be true. Java confirmed it, too. After the door finally shut, and the visitors were gone, I roamed aimlessly around the house while my heart floated gracefully. Still sensing his man energy on my arm, I cleaned up the variety of snacks that loosely decorated the kitchen counter. Java looked up at me inquisitively, cocked her head, and swayed her rear end with joy.

"He's a good one, isn't he Girlie?!"

Wag, wag, bigger wag.

Things changed that night, and as Java and I laid quietly on the couch, I felt my heart grow freer and skip a beat with joy. Java rolled over onto her back and stretched, while I cradled her head in my arm, and listened to her steady breathing become a much steadier snore. I went to bed with an open heart of gratitude, and thanked the Universe profusely for bringing Allen into my life. Drifting off to sleep, I felt Java jump onto the bed with me, then plop down lazily and moan with content.

The melody of songbirds roused me from my slumber, as the warmth of the fall sun illuminated the new day. Getting ready for work, I felt very centered inside and replayed the events of the weekend, over and over, until they rested quietly within me. Grabbing my lunch, I locked Java in her crate, then glanced again at the wishbone twig that was still balancing itself perfectly on my bookshelf.

"I'll see you later, sweetie," I said to Java, as I tossed her a biscuit and blew her a kiss.

Locking the door behind me, I smiled as I skipped down the walkway toward my car. I felt like I had a new secret in my heart!

Nearing my SUV, I was unaware that a huge surprise awaited me. Whistling happily to the driver's side, I grabbed my key then looked up to notice that my entire sunroof was shattered into tiny, little pieces—blanketing the front seat of my car with danger. Hundreds of chunks of glass glistened sharply in the sunlight as I looked around and wondered what had happened. Lying about six feet from the back bumper was a four-foot tree branch, but there wasn't a scratch or dent anywhere on my car. As I put the key in the door, I peered inside and spotted a two-inch piece of wood in the back seat among more scattered chunks of glass.

Can a four-foot branch fall off a tree, bounce off my sunroof before shattering it, miss the whole car entirely, then land six feet away? Anything's possible.

When something that messy occurs, there's not much else you can do in the moment but laugh. Grabbing a dirty, pink dog towel from the back of the car, I folded it underneath me, then drove two blocks to work on a crunchy blanket of glass.

167

CHAPTER ELEVEN

PEACE

"Contentment does not exist in heaping up more fuel, but in taking away some fire."

~ Thomas Fuller

Staring at the blank page on my computer screen, the word "PEACE" echoed freely in my empty mind. It's not that I haven't experienced peace, or couldn't write about it, but something wasn't clicking. Call it writer's block or divine intervention, but I wasn't meant to write a chapter about peace.

As I looked down at the curious Plott Hound lying by my side, clarity presented itself. I thought to myself, "Here I am, writing an entire book about my interactions with Java, and I haven't even stopped long enough to ask for her input."

"You wanna write this chapter, Little Brown Bear?"

I smiled into Java's chestnut brown eyes, and caught a slight glimpse of eagerness in her gaze. I stroked the side of her once completely brown muzzle that was now starting to grey, and let out another deep exhale. In the five years we've been together, Java and I have learned how to communicate telepathically with one another. Here I was, asking her advice, and trusting what I felt in response. My mind remained an empty slate as I laid next to Java for what seemed like a long time. In actuality, it was just a brief moment that stopped long enough for me to know what to do.

When you're extremely connected with another being on a spiritual level, it's quite simple to feel what they feel, and intuitively *become* them for a stretch of time. After that simple exchange, I wrote like I was on fire. The fire wasn't coming from me, however. It came straight from Java.

In Java's own words....
"Change? Oh boy, was there change!! Things *really* started to change even days after she met Allen. Sage was singing, dancing, smiling, laughing, and playing with me more. She

was absolutely giddy and goofy if you ask me, but she also seemed to be a lot more settled—settled in the same kind of way she asked *me* to be for so long. She was working out her muscles in the morning with yoga, lifting weights, and writing in her journal every day. In between dancing, singing and being happy, she'd stop to kiss me or do those new circular TTouches on my body with her hands. I liked it because it made me feel relaxed and quiet. Within a week of the first emails they sent back and forth, Allen called Sage on the phone. That's all it took.

They were on the phone *constantly*. Sometimes I'd be sound asleep and they were still talking until way after the moon was out.

Don't humans ever sleep when they're in love?

Speaking of love, I know Allen told Sage he loved her on the phone because I felt it. She told me later that it fell out of his mouth during one of their phone conversations. Allen gets really excited and can't wait to do stuff sometimes. I'm the same way. Sage told Allen she loved him also because she really did. I could tell they loved each other. Then, she told Allen she couldn't wait to tell him that she loved him in person, although she really wanted to. He said he couldn't keep it inside any longer either because the love was bursting out all over the place. I think that's super sweet. I'm glad the love fell out.

In no time, Allen started to visit us on the weekends. Almost every Friday night, he'd drive from Minneapolis to Madison, then on Sundays he'd drive from Madison to Minneapolis. That's a lot of driving, and a lot of love. It was great when Allen came to visit us but I felt sad to see him leave.

Why did he have to live so far away?

It seemed like a lifetime from the time I saw him until he came back the next time. Sage told me it was only five days, but I couldn't help myself. I got so filled up with joy that I almost *POPPED* each time he walked in the door!

I thought it was funny how I already knew what a good kisser he was. I kissed him first, you know. It was easy for me to figure out that Allen was really cool and not scary, but Sage needed to figure that out on her own. It takes humans so much longer to figure stuff out before they feel okay to kiss. She was really happy when Allen was around, and although I got less attention, it seemed to make me feel more peaceful inside. She wasn't so fidgety, anxious, and worrying when he was near us. Plus, he was fun, peaceful, and nice. Sometimes I'd drop my tennis ball in his suitcase on Sunday nights just to see if he'd notice before he packed up. He always did. Then, we'd play one last round of fetch before he left for the week, and I'd sneak in another kiss right before he walked out the door.

I could tell Sage was happy by how light and bouncy she seemed. Allen was a blast to be around because he was really happy, too. It felt like home to snuggle between them while they talked or kissed. Sometimes I felt left out so I'd wiggle my way in between and make them laugh. I liked to sit on his lap, kiss his mustache and nibble on his nose. I could tell right away how much he loved me.

Who wouldn't? I'm very, very pretty.
I'm the Tremendous Stupendous Princess Girl!

A few weeks after these two lovebirds met, Sage and I left in the car to go to my third TTouch Training in Cincinnati, Ohio. You'd think we were leaving forever, because two days before we left, a package arrived from Allen. Inside the neatly taped box was a used green sweatshirt with his smell on it. I wondered why he would send her a used sweatshirt but I was really happy to smell him. Then, I figured out why. Sage sat in the car the entire trip to Cincinnati, sniffing and snorting her sleeve while she drove with a stupid grin on her face. I rested my head on her shoulder because I missed him, too. He really *does* smell nice!

Car rides are really fun because I don't have to do anything special. The blink, blink, blinker sound always gets me going though because I know we're about to stop for one reason or another.

Taco Bell! Taco Bell! Taco Bell!

I don't understand why you have to slow down and throw money out the window to drive on the roads in Illinois. It seems like a waste to me, but it does make a fun sound and everyone else is doing it so it must be okay.

When we got to Cincinnati, all of a sudden I remembered. The hotel smelled the same and all of my TTouch aunties were there—Aunt Kathy, Aunt Kelly, Aunt Judy, and Edie Jane! I had memories of humans strapping me up with all sorts of unfamiliar equipment, and practicing touching me and moving me around cones and stuff.

Remind me why we're doing this?
Oh yeah, so we can feel better about ourselves.

Once we got into Session Three it felt a lot better because the people remembered me, and so did the animals. They cut me a lot of slack at those trainings because I sometimes have sudden outbursts. I don't quite have those under control yet. My stomach feels upset when I get scared and I try really hard to hold it in, but it busts out sometimes. I'm learning. I'm also feeling more settled and relaxed, and it feels really nice. These trainings are challenging for me, but I also feel a lot of love and respect. Nobody reaches for the top of my head or stares at me, and it's the only place where I feel like I truly fit in—like who I am is okay. There's this guy in the class who I like a lot. His name is Dana. He can actually *talk* to me and understand what I say back to him. I mean he can *really* talk to me. People can talk to animals you know. It's just that most of them forgot how. I love him a lot. He loves me, too.

Who wouldn't?

When Sage leaves to go to another room, Dana sometimes holds my leash. He talks to me then touches me to make sure my skin is loose. My skin gets tight when I get scared, but he helps me remember to loosen it up. I can breathe easily when I'm with Dana because I feel trusted, respected and accepted.

The hard part is when I have to teach a lesson to everyone in the class. I don't like to be the center of attention. I know some people would think otherwise, but I'm actually kind of shy. It doesn't always appear that way when I'm lunging, snarling, and carrying on.

The times I like the most are when people practice their TTouches on my body. It makes me feel unbelievably loved and cared for, and I can feel myself settling into a place that's new and calm. It's kind of like my body feels alive, yet soft and yummy at the same time. I've learned a lot about how I like to be touched, and where it feels the best on my body.

I try hard to teach the humans, but it takes them such a long time to learn. They don't always pay a lot of attention to what I'm trying to tell them, like how I yawn or lick my lips when I'm feeling uneasy. They usually get distracted because they're thinking so much, so I lean over and bring them back to the moment with a kiss.

Slurrrpp!

There's this thing they do at TTouch Trainings called the Confidence Course or Playground for Higher Learning. It's pretty cool. You get to walk over ladders, around cones, through a labyrinth, and up and down ramps. I like it a lot. When I'm in the Confidence Course I can feel my brain working. It's kind of like a math test, and I feel kind of fancy and smart. We walk slowly through the Confidence Course, and I actually notice where my body is going. When I walk slowly, I can pay attention to how I stand, and whether I feel good about it or not. It's kind of like having someone hold your paw so you don't get scared, and can be more successful.

I felt like a pro at the third TTouch Training, and it was great to see Edie Jane again. I remembered her easily when she touched me because her hands were filled with love and understanding. I could feel it. I started to feel better about myself and not quite so anxious and stressed. So did Sage.

She kept calling Allen the entire week we were gone, but it was okay. She even showed me a picture she brought for our hotel room where he was only wearing his underwear. That's weird. Humans spend *far* too much time thinking, feeling and wondering.

When class was done each day, I was exhausted. It felt nice to get rid of the harness, head collar and TTouch Body Wrap that covered my body, and lie on the bed and watch cable. We don't have cable at home. I liked spending the nights alone with Sage, and I think the Travel Channel® is cool. The days were hard for both of us, but we always learned a lot. Plus, the more we worked together with TTouch, the better I felt about myself.

After we got home from the training it seemed like things got even closer between Sage and Allen. He was visiting every weekend but then she started to cry when he left to drive home. I felt bad for her, and kissed her tears away a lot of the time. Overall, she seemed more peaceful than I'd ever seen her, but I could tell by the way I felt inside how much her heart loved Allen. She loved him as much as she loved me, and boy, I sure knew how much she loved me!

Winter came and went, because I remember playing in the cold and snow, but then things got muddy and warmer. As the seasons changed, Allen kept visiting us, and then we'd all get sad when he left to go back to Minneapolis. It was hard because we had become a family.

During the spring, Sage and I went to Cincinnati again for our fourth TTouch Training. The weather was getting warmer, so I knew Sage was going to be done with school for the summer pretty soon. I don't really remember a lot of details about the fourth TTouch Training except how excited I felt to see my friends, and how much easier it seemed. Oh, and that I got to ride in Edie Jane's car to the coffee shop!

Each time I returned to a new TTouch Training, I felt stronger and more confident. I liked watching people smile at me. Finally, other people wanted to take my leash and do some work with me. For so long, people seemed to be afraid, and that made me sad. But as I got older and was doing more TTouch work, I started to feel better about myself. I guess I felt more peaceful. I could focus while I was walking instead of being so stressed out that I panted and pulled harder. It was really hard for me to go slow at first, but the world looks *so* beautiful when you actually notice what's around you.

Try it! The dogs in the class were still kind of scary to me, but I had fewer outbursts and slept a lot more. Eventually, I was able to relax because I knew Sage was going to watch out for me. For such a long time it seemed like she was way too distracted or uncoordinated. It seemed like *I* was the one who needed to do all the watching. What a relief to settle into the passenger seat and let someone else steer the ship.

We practiced TTouch work a lot together at home, and Sage was busy practicing with other animals, too. It seemed that every day I learned how to settle more, and I was also able to lie in a different room by myself without getting worried. That made me feel kind of grown up. When Sage left to go to work, I still needed to be in a metal cage, but it was okay because I could see out and I felt safer there. A lot of times she'd take me to her school so I could play with the kids during art class. It was so much fun to be around kids and run free. Kids are *much* cooler than adults. They seem to love me no matter what, and they understand me better than some adults do. I also amazed the kids with all of my tricks. I know a lot of tricks. Would you like to see them? I'm very good at doing tricks.

When the weather got warmer it felt like something was changing at our house. School usually ended when the weather got hot which meant that Sage and I got to spend a ton of time together in the yard, and in the hammock. But I saw her packing things in boxes, so I kind of wondered what was happening. She seemed even happier and more peaceful, yet she was throwing some of our stuff away, and Allen sometimes left with our plants and furniture in his truck, too. I didn't pay much attention until my favorite chair got carried out the door.

Excuse me? That was my chair! Did anyone ask me if it could leave the house? Hmmph!

More things got packed into boxes, and Allen seemed really happy to carry our stuff to his red pick-up truck and drive away. Humans sure have a lot of stuff.

Where was he going with ours?

Even though the house was getting emptier, and things were kind of messy, everything felt settled in the house — even me. There was a kind of excitement at our house that hadn't been there before, and I think it had something to do with Allen and Sage's love.

Although it seemed like forever, I guess it was only a few days of moving boxes until she finally told me what was happening. We were selling our house and moving to Minneapolis to be with Allen."

Okay.

CHAPTER TWELVE

GROWTH

"When the most important things in our life happen we quite often do not know, at the moment, what is going on."

~ C.S. Lewis

My heart knew exactly what was going on—mutual love. It made me quit my job, sell my house, and move to Minneapolis, Minnesota after eight months of a deep, intense, long-distance relationship with Allen. Although it may sound like an easy decision, it certainly wasn't. It was one of those times in your life when you can feel in your heart where growth is an option you need to take, but you need to risk running through fear to get there. I was scared, but my belly felt soft, calm, and settled. My house sold 48 hours after it was listed on the market, and that seemed like a clear sign I was heading the right direction.

Two weeks after the school year ended, and the date of my house closing, I sat face-to-face with my school superintendent and resigned from my nine-year position as an elementary art instructor. Sitting outside the administration building was Allen's pick-up truck, filled with my last load of stuff, and my sweet girl, Java.

As I walked away from a life that felt familiar, I neared the truck with a huge smile. Java was sitting in the driver's seat, sniffing out the window, and wagging her entire body with joy. Sitting side-by-side with Java in the front seat, I felt like a stronger woman with a gentler dog. We were on our way to starting a new chapter in our lives.

My head swirled with memories during the drive from Madison to Minneapolis. It had been just over a year since Java and I had driven to Minneapolis for our very first TTouch Training, and where we had been in such a short time was challenging, heart wrenching, breathtaking, and freeing. And now, I was turning a huge page in my life to follow my heart. Passing through cities along the way, I was reminded of friends, family, and past love relationships that I was leaving behind.

Changing lanes, I looked up to see the rear view mirror reflecting back the last of my personal belongings, strapped precariously in the bed of Allen's pick-up. Feelings of excitement and uncertainty about the future filled my body, as Java laid her heavy, brown head on my lap and fell sound asleep. Snoring loudly, she added a steady sound to the choppy rhythm of the tires on the highway. I smiled down, remembering a time not very long ago when her entire body fit on my lap.

Driving into rush hour traffic in Minneapolis, I felt and looked like the Beverly Hillbillies with a truckload of odd items strapped together in a pick-up. As the truck slowed, Java lifted her head off my lap, then popped it out the window to smell our new city. With summer breezes flowing through the cab of the truck, our eyes scanned the metropolitan skyline for opportunities. Reaching down, I turned on the radio, and began flipping through stations as traffic slowed to a halt. Java's entire head was out the window, ears flopping in the breeze, and she was completely content to be somewhere new. Me, I needed to find a radio station that made me feel like this was home. Intention is everything, so within minutes, I landed on the soothing, tropical sounds of the Caribbean.

Okay, I can live here.

Traffic let up a bit, and Java and I were only a few miles away from our new home. I felt nervous, excited and filled with questions while Java continued to smell the world in peace. Rounding the corner of Gray's Bay Boulevard in Minnetonka, Allen met us with smiles and hugs in the driveway of his tiny Swiss-style cottage on Gray's Bay. If you've ever taken a leap that huge, the first hug of your new life is indescribable. Hopping out of the car, I wrapped my entire body in Allen's arms and held him tight.

Java wagged, hopped, and whined uncontrollably from the truck, just to remind us not to forget her—as if that were possible.

"Hey, Girlie!" Allen said, as he grabbed Java's leash, then sprinted with her around her new yard.

I headed up the stairs to the cottage with a potted fern in my arms, and watched Allen and Java run, jump, and laugh together. As I turned my head toward the front window, I caught reflections of my belongings in his house and gasped. I'm not sure it was necessarily good or bad, it just sunk in that I had really done it. I had finally become a woman who listened to her heart, and took action.

"I love you, sweet girl," Allen said strongly to me, as he and Java flew through the door, and I flew into his arms again.

Looking back at him deeply, our bodies and souls connected, and I responded completely, "I love you, too."

Java adjusted quicker to change than any of us. She easily found her favorite place on the futon couch in front of the huge picture windows in order to keep a watchful eye on the fancy people walking past. It didn't take Java or I very long to check out every nook and cranny of our new space. The 600 square foot cottage was adorable, but the big decision before us was where to put a 36" x 40" x 48" dog crate without having to use it for a dining room table. Java solved the dilemma.

After a full day of unpacking, Allen and I wanted to leave the cottage to catch our breath, run some errands, and have some time alone. Cursing the huge dog crate, I put it in the only place available—the hallway—and succumbed to the fact that we had a tiny space and a big dog.

Locking Java in her crate, I gave her a treat, told her where we were going, when we'd be home, and what I expected of her while we were gone. As Allen and I walked down the front porch stairway to his truck, Java let out the same huge howl she did the night Veta left us. She had made her decision clear.

"She wants to get out," I told Allen hesitantly, as I wondered how he would handle this challenging dog in *his* space now.

"Let's let her out!" Allen responded cheerily, then ran up the front steps and unlocked the door.

As he walked over to Java's crate and freed her, my heart warmed with joy.

"You gotta behave, Girlie. This is rental property,"

Allen explained in detail to Java as she circled his feet with a half-destroyed toy in her mouth, trying her best to listen. Then Allen walked to the kitchen, grabbed another treat for Java and told her to 'get in her spot.' Java looked back at Allen with confusion (so did I), then ran to the futon and sat down. He smiled at both of us, handed Java the treat, told her where we were going, when we'd be back, and that it was now her job to watch the house.

Heading out the door for the first time with Java free in the house was harder for me than anyone. Allen reassured me all the way to his truck that Java would be absolutely fine on her own for twenty minutes as long as I wasn't busy wringing my hands with worry. Every few minutes,

Allen looked over at me, held my hand tighter, and said, "She's fine."

Within days, we left for half an hour, an hour, and then finally a couple of hours. Each time we returned, everything was still in its same place in the house, and Java greeted us with a full body wag at the door. Well, except once when we caught her standing on top of the dining room table to get a better view of the neighbors.

The first week Java and I moved in with Allen, our adventures began. Turning over in bed, I saw the clock blinking, and the normal rumble of the refrigerator was now silenced. Being without electricity isn't a big deal, but as I got up to look out the window, as I normally do first thing in he morning, I laughed at what I saw. Covering our entire yard, all the way to the street, was a brand new lake that hadn't been there the night before. Heavy rains, and living in low ground, we were prime targets for catastrophe.

Waking Allen up with my chuckle, he of course asked what was so funny, then looked out the window to confirm. He couldn't help laughing, too. Then Java came bounding into the bedroom, hopped up on the bed between Allen and I, and wondered which one of us was going to let her outside to potty. She obviously hadn't looked out the window.

Flooding can be very challenging when you have a 60 pound dog who's afraid of water. With Allen around, creative problem solving was free entertainment. Without discussion, Allen jumped up, grabbed a pair of royal blue swim trunks, and called Java to the door. Following closely behind, my wonder turned to love as I watched Allen pick Java up like a big sack of groceries, then asked me to open the door. Java relaxed completely in his arms, as Allen explained in detail to her how fun it was going to be that she wouldn't have to swim through a lake to go potty. Standing at the window in pajamas, I watched the man I loved and the dog I loved moving toward higher ground together. It was a sweet opportunity to witness an unconditional act, and it was more than obvious how much Java and Allen adored one another. We were *all* blessed with love. The flood lasted a few days, and Allen continued to carry Java to higher ground without ever thinking twice. She was *his* dog now, too.

During the flood days I was enrolled in a TTouch for Humans workshop taught by Linda Tellington-Jones. My goal was to use TTouch work not only with animals, but also people—hopefully kids. With only two more TTouch Trainings remaining before I was certified to work with companion animals, I was eager to use what I had learned, and ready to get my animal training business, Dancing Porcupine, on the map in Minnesota. Starting a new business in a new city, can be a bit challenging so I set my intention to research the market, then educate that market about Tellington TTouch®. Although TTouch had been around for almost thirty years, it wasn't commonplace in the Midwest, and I wanted it to be. Here I was, starting a business while trying to nurture a new relationship in a city that was unfamiliar. I had my work cut out for me.

When the lake transformed back into a muddy front yard, Allen and I took Java outside on a leash to relieve herself. We also used a cable tie-out in the ground to give her more freedom and privacy. I had gotten so used to a half acre fenced yard, so I was bummed because I felt like she was so restricted, but Java could have cared less.

Again, she adjusted really well and very quickly, only running to the end of the cable and ripping the tie- out from the soft ground once before we used our brains. Across the yard the metal corkscrew danced at the end of the cable, trailing faithfully behind Java as she ran into the neighbor's yard to say 'hello.'

Allen, Java and I took more walks than we had taken before, and our new family now included a third party with bigger muscles to make walks easier. It felt incredibly freeing to go for a walk with Java at my side and someone else holding the leash. I found myself actually breathing and enjoying walks again because Allen and Java shared a beautiful understanding. She pulled, and he stopped. He pulled, and she stopped. And when both of them couldn't stand the slow pace anymore, they took off sprinting at high speed together—down the street, through the woods, across fields and streams—whatever it took to make it fun. Java was lucky to have a guy that cared so much about her well-being. I was, too.

There's something beautiful about a new romance when you're in your late thirties and have both been married before. It's in relationships that we grow the most if we allow it. But it's not always easy to grow. Sometimes we push, pull, stomp our feet, and run away. When we open our hearts to each moment that comes along as a gift to learn and try again, we find the purity of love. Allen and I were deeply connected—spiritually, emotionally, physically and mentally—more than either one of us had felt before with a partner. We were a family.

Allen would often suggest taking Java somewhere new or else he'd hop in his truck and say, "Come on, Girlie. Let's go!" Off the two of them would go on a top-secret adventure, sharing very little of their classified information when they returned to home base.

The first summer we spent in Minnesota, Java experienced more newness than in the first 2-1/2 years of her life. We had frequent bonfires, new people visiting, more walks, more playing, more cuddling, more freedom, understanding, and love. It still blows my mind how easily she adjusted. It was *me* who struggled. Once I got to Minnesota it felt painfully obvious that leaving my familiar life behind made me feel ungrounded. I'd left my friends, family, history, career, and my self—by choice.

Who was I in this new city?
Where was I?

I felt lost and confused, like a banana without a peel or a cone without ice cream—or a chewed up piece of bubble gum waiting patiently on the hot pavement to be carried somewhere else by the bottom of a giant shoe. Being ungrounded is a crappy feeling. You go from day to day just existing but not really sure about how to make each day fulfilling. Nothing seems to fit right. When I first became divorced, I went through a bit of the same—learning to get my sea legs back—but now I lived in a new city, with new people, and new opportunities.

Not long after I moved to Minnesota, my self-esteem started to take a nosedive, and it took me off guard. When I left my job as a teacher, I lost a part of my identity. Leaving the city I grew up in, I lost a large part of my memories and history. Leaving my colleagues, friends, and family, I left my large support system and relied more on Allen.

Then, there was moving to a new city. I got lost nearly every day while driving—not knowing which direction my house was to get home. Making frequent tearful calls to Allen's work, he'd patiently help me get back on track. In Minnesota there's no 'left or right' when you ask for directions, but rather north, south, east and west. I felt inadequate because I didn't know which direction my house sat on a compass. If time allowed, Allen would draw me a map for the day on a tiny slip of colorful paper, then kiss my forehead for luck.

It didn't dawn on me before I uprooted myself how difficult it might be for me to transition. I anticipated I would struggle emotionally to let go of the past and ground myself in a new place, but I wasn't prepared for the depth of the struggle. It was hard to watch Allen go to work each day while I stayed home and tried to promote my animal business, Dancing Porcupine. I felt lonely and ungrounded, and wanted to spend more time getting to know Allen before we jumped into reality. I know now that nurturing a new relationship is vital, but we continued our lives as if nothing had actually changed other than we were now in the same house. Allen and I were silly in love but had gone from fantasy to reality without paying much attention. Our relationship changed, and it took us both awhile to realize how much.

Allen was very supportive of my struggles, however, he also found himself lost about how to help an independent woman without overstepping either of our boundaries. At the same time, he was trying to figure out how to nurture a relationship and balance himself as well. It was a dance we both chose to engage in but neither of us knew how to dance this one without stepping on toes. In hindsight, we needed help, but we weren't aware.

Soon, I started to promote my business the only way I knew how—by making cold calls and driving around posting posters for free Tellington TTouch® demonstrations. I carried business cards for Dancing Porcupine wherever I went, and was often found talking to someone about a new pet or a pet with issues of some sort. Next, I found the animal community. I met other women animal trainers and business owners for lunch to brainstorm, share stories, and give and receive support.

Within very little time, I felt like being an animal trainer in Minneapolis was a great fit for me. Things were falling into place one by one, and then one more piece appeared. At the end of July, Java and I were preparing to head to our fifth TTouch Training in Cincinnati. This time, I packed two suitcases—one with human clothes and a separate one of Body Wraps, harnesses, head collars, TTouch books, case studies and journals. Lying on the bed together the night before our trip, I chatted on the phone with my TTouch friend, Kelly, as something spectacular occurred. Java spoke to me telepathically, and I heard what she had to say.

For quite some time I received words, images, and feelings from animals who I worked with and wondered if I was nuts. After talking with a number of animal communicators, including my sister, I was reassured to the fact that I wasn't nuts but rather blessed. For almost an entire year, animals tapped into *me* but I was unable to tap into *them*. In other words, the animals realized before I did that I could hear them, so they started talking to me first. Yes, like Dr. Doolittle.

Java's first words chilled me to the bone. There's something about hearing the voice of your own animal talk to you. I'm sure you've experienced a feeling where you absolutely *knew* there was a stronger connection yet nothing could explain it—a time when you looked into your animal's eyes and it seemed like you could read their mind. You can. They can read yours, too.

"I'm scared," Java said to me in a fast, quiet voice that showed apprehension.

I paused and went back to my conversation with Kelly, an accomplished animal communicator herself.

"Java just told me she's scared," I said to Kelly with the same voice of apprehension Java had uttered.

"Cool! What's she afraid of?" Kelly bounced back with excitement.

"I don't know. I was afraid to ask her," I responded quickly. We both laughed aloud.

The next morning when our wheels started to head to Session Five in Cincinnati, I loaded the tape player in my car with Penelope Smith's series on telepathic communication with animals (*The Interspecies Telepathic Connection;* Pegasus Publications). What I learned was that 99% of communicating with animals is about believing—believing it's possible and believing in yourself. Within minutes of driving and listening, I learned how to open myself to Java and ask her to open herself to me. Boy, was I in for an earful.

For the next hour and a half she talked and talked, while I kept myself open to listening and hearing. Actually, she yelled and screamed. Java told me how angry she was at me for leaving her with the dogs who attacked her, how she wanted to hunt and play more games, and that she wanted more freedom overall. She pretty much read me the riot act for about one hundred miles, and I didn't know what to do. Finally, I called my sister, Stephanie, for advice. As a public speaker, Steph can talk to humans well, but as an animal communicator, she can also talk with animals.

"Steph, I just connected with Java and she's been yelling at me for an hour and a half. How do I shut it off?"

Stephanie giggled on the other end of the line, paused, and responded gently, "You can't. She's been quiet for almost three years. Listen to what she has to say."

So, listen I did. Then something more incredible happened. I started to believe in myself during the drive. Asking Java specific questions, I trusted in the answers, and by the time we arrived in Cincinnati, we were both exhausted and even more bonded. I felt like I understood her better and was excited to start my second to last TTouch Training with our newfound relationship. With hugs, wags, and kisses abounding, we got to the Econo Lodge® to see our mutual friends and Java's aunties—Kelly, Judy and Kathy. These three women took Java under their wings from the moment they met her almost a year before. They loved her, understood, respected, and cared for her as if she was their own. The bond between my TTouch colleagues and I was getting stronger as well, and each night after the training, we found ourselves wrapped in deep conversation over a bottle of wine, a smorgasbord of food, and an exhausted Plott Hound hogging the bed for love, attention, and a pillow. Kathy and Judy couldn't stop themselves from kissing and touching Java, and it warmed my heart to see other people love her and understand her as much as I did. Java ate it up.

Kelly and I shared a much quieter understanding. She taught me how to be freer with Java like she was with her beautiful, senior dog, Kita. Kelly also showed me how some dogs, even though they might be muscle-bound like Java, enjoy light, gentle touch with a lot of breaks in between.

Most beings enjoy being touched in some way. If you watch how animals (and humans) respond to the way you touch them, and where you touch them, it's quite interesting. For some, a light touch may be soothing. For others, a light touch may be stimulating or even startling. Think about the places on your body that feel safe enough for a stranger to touch. How about a friend or a lover? Some beings enjoy stronger touch, scratching, rubbing or patting. Yet some enjoy slow, light and gentle. It's this beautiful balance that we all have the ability to harvest with another being, and all it really takes is paying attention. Are they moving further away or closer? Are they breathing? People and animals aren't much different from one another, but what I love about animals is that they're completely honest. When you allow an animal to come and go on their own accord, they'll often move closer when they feel safe, respected, loved, and trusted. They'll also move away when something doesn't feel right. Many humans will tolerate things that don't particularly feel nice for fear of hurting someone's feelings, due to the inability to ask for what they want instead. It's sometimes difficult as humans to ask for what we want, yet animals do it all the time.

When they need space, they take it. When they want to be close, they get close. When they're hungry, they eat, and tired, they sleep. They don't worry anywhere near as much as we do about what others think about them. With my TTouch Training almost coming to a close after a year and a half, Java and I were ready to continue to teach and learn. I felt like my entire life had changed since the last time we had all gathered together to work with animals. It had. I was no longer hanging sexy photos of Allen in my hotel room, but rather calling him at lunch break to tell him how much I loved him, and to see how his day was going. At night, we often did our own thing—knowing we were connected by our hearts—yet he always called to wish me 'sweet dreams' and see how Java's day had been at the training.

Session Five was taught by a TTouch instructor from the west coast, Debby Potts. Debby taught me the importance of breathing and being in the moment when you're working with animals or humans. Dogs can tell when you hold your breath. So can people. I learned to exhale my inhales, and watch Java's rib cage move up and down with ease. I learned that when her ribs were moving, she was more relaxed, and when her ribs stood still, she was ready to lunge. I learned that I hold my breath when I'm concentrating, and that my hands get cold and my stomach gets tight when I forget to exhale. Then, I learned to whisper quietly when I'm working with an animal because it's forces you to breathe. Plus, they pay closer attention.

We don't often notice how much breathing affects our every day living. When we hold our breath, we're denying our body the oxygen it needs to be healthy. When we exhale, we rid our body of toxins and prepare to inhale another breath of life. When we become aware of our breath, we can make a conscious choice to relax, release, and let go. Conscious breathing brings us to the moment, and cleanses our body, mind and soul.

Exhale.

Java learned to breathe easier when I learned to pay attention. If I noticed Java holding her breath, I'd check my own breathing and let out a big exhale. It often reminded her to do the same. Java and I became more centered with our bodies, mind, and spirit during Session Five, and my snarly snapper was turning into a Zen dog. We learned how to put it all together at this training—touch, movement, breathing, and intention.

At the start of each day, Debby would signal the beginning of class with a crystal clear '*Ding!*' of a brass, singing bowl. Java's attention turned in an instant toward Debby as if to say, "Yes, Sensei. I am focused and ready to begin."

The mornings were spent learning how to become more aware—to slow down, observe without judgment, and be conscious in the moment. Java and I were both changing and feeling better about ourselves.

Journal Entry
7/21/03 – Touch Training: Session 5, Day 1

Java was non-reactive to both humans and dogs and lying down right away. She's nosing me when she gets worried, and wagging her tail a lot. She's crossed a huge milestone, and I've also noticed how warm my hands have been all morning. Java is going to Dana a lot for reassurance—even jumped into his lap at one point when she heard a tiny kitten meow. Great progress for Java already. She's lying down asleep at 11 a.m.

By lunchtime, Kelly made me a huge proposition. "Let's let Kita and Java meet each other. You wanna?" Kelly giggled and bounced.

Responding nervously, I succumbed to peer pressure. Kelly easily understood dog language, so she suggested we go outside to the large fenced area and put Kita inside a smaller fenced area within. She knew Kita would give very clear calming signals (licking lips, yawning, looking away, moving her body to the side, sniffing the ground) to show Java she wasn't a threat. How Java would respond, I didn't know. With tall fences between them, I let go of Java's leash. growth: *Unlocking the Inner Door*

Journal Entry
7/21/03 – TTouch Training: Session 5, Day 1

We let Kita and Java outside in two separate fenced areas for the first time today. Java was off leash and able to move at her own pace. With her nose down, Java walked into the yard, then up to Kita's face, wagged her tail and quickly walked away. Java then walked back to Kita—this time appropriately approaching her from the side. Kita didn't make any eye contact whatsoever with Java. Java bounced around in joy and ran to the door to go inside. This was an incredibly freeing and successful experience for both Java and I!

Kelly, Kita, Java and I headed back into the training room, and a group of wondering eyeballs met us at the door.

"Well? How'd it go?" Judy and Kathy asked simultaneously, while Kelly giggled, then smiled at me.

"It was incredible," I replied with the joy of a brand new parent watching their kid achieve something that once seemed out of reach.

As the training progressed, more of my colleagues were working with Java, while I worked with other dogs. I began to realize how freeing it was to watch her grow from a distance. I beamed with pride when Java eyeballed me from across the room, and was still able to keep her body and mind under control. We were both growing in leaps and bounds—feeling freer than we'd ever felt, and more connected than we'd ever been. In every spare moment, I called or wrote Allen to tell him of our progress or just to hear his voice. I couldn't wait to get home to him, yet I was also in bliss at this training. Session Five was the only training which didn't bring me to tears for some reason or another, and I felt spiritually stronger than ever before. I knew my path was clear.

After learning how to communicate telepathically with Java, our whole world opened up, but sometimes I needed to be reminded that it was possible. At lunchtime and during shelter visits, I boarded Java at the facility in a kennel area because I needed to be dogless for awhile. She was quite anxious in a dog run, often jumping repeatedly in the air, panting, and whining to get out. I felt bad for her, yet I wasn't sure how to help her through this. Allen knew. Calling him for moral support before lunch one day, he offered a gem in return.

"We're working at a shelter this afternoon, and I have to kennel Java. She gets so stressed out, and I feel badly for her," I explained to Allen as he listened intently on the other end of the line, then responded wisely,

"Why don't you just talk to her about it?"

In doing so, Java opened up immediately about the details of her life before I got her. She shared with me the scary parts of her life before eleven weeks old—telling me how she had lived among rows of kennels at a breeding facility, and that it had been very difficult for her. Java went on to explain how her wire kennel door was hit repeatedly with a large, wooden stick and how jumpy it made her feel.

Continuing on, she shared that the person on the end of the stick was a tall, dark-haired man with a mustache and a red baseball hat, and that his dark brown boot had kicked her right hip at one point. She shared stories of lying on the soiled cement in the kennel near her male litter mate who had died, and how she felt blamed for the puppy's death by the tall man with dark hair. She associated all boarding kennels with her first, unpleasant incident when she was only a few weeks old, and became filled with worry and anxiety anytime I left her among the rows, and rows of kennels.

The more open I was to receiving, the more Java continued to share with me. Thoughts, images, and feelings found their way from Java to me, as she explained how the sound in boarding kennels is too loud, that she can't sleep, and how she gets worried the other dogs are going to 'get her'. I assured her the chain link fences prevented anyone from 'getting her' (and vice versa), and that she was actually very safe. After that explanation, Java got very excited, then asked me to go into her kennel with her so she could show me around and we could have lunch together.

Wouldn't you crawl into a 4' x 6' cement kennel with your dog to eat lunch if they asked?

Opening the chain link door, Java and I entered into her kennel space together, as I locked the gate behind us. Java ran in circles, bounced up and down a few times, then ran through the doggie door to the outside run. A brief moment passed before Java's happy, brown head peeked back at me through the tiny door that led to her outside world.

I could see her entire body wagging from the look in her eyes, as she looked back at me then asked, "Aren't you coming?"

At 5'10" tall it's quite a challenge to squeeze through an 18" x 24" doggie door with grace, but for Java I'd do anything. With my head to the ground and my butt in the air, I squeezed my tall, slim body clumsily through the doggie door, and then flopped myself into Java's outdoor world. Remember the part in the Wizard of Oz where Dorothy opens the door and it goes from black and white to color? Crawling through that doggie door showed me a colorful part of Java's world that I never would have seen had I not made the effort.

Brushing myself off, I smiled at Java as she showed an incredible look of delight and amazement on her face. I think she was surprised that I actually made it through that tiny space. Her eyes glistened wide with exuberance as her entire body wagged clumsily with joy and freedom. Running to the back of the run, she showed me how beautiful and serene it was. She *did* have a great view! Java and I sat amidst cement and chain link for almost half an hour, and shared a hummus, Swiss cheese and tomato sandwich together. It was the quietest I had seen her in a kennel, and also the most excited and grateful I had seen her. Sometimes all it takes is a little flexibility to understand your dog better. By taking the time to talk with Java, and listen to her, I was able to help dissolve her fears.

By the fourth day of the training, Java was asked to be a 'Demo Dog.' Her job was to model and demonstrate how to use ropes to create both a simple harness, and a Double Diamond—two methods of guiding dogs to have better body awareness, balance and self-control. Java rose to the occasion—standing still as a marble statue—while the instructor (Debby) suited Java up in a variety of fancy, rope configurations and explained how a simple tool such as a rope could be so beneficial. The harness was a fast way to contain a wiggly dog, like at a shelter, and the Double Diamond was an even better way to help control the front and back end of a dog who spins. I felt like a proud parent as well as a good animal trainer, while Java calmly wore her purple rope outfit, and rested her muzzle on the chair in front of her until Debby was 'done with her'.

At break time, Java greeted other dogs with tail wags from a distance, and whined when she saw greyhounds running in a nearby field. Back at the hotel, she greeted Kita with a quick bump of her nose to Kita's neck then ran quickly away with a look of pride and accomplishment. She was making better choices when she was close to dogs, and I was feeling calmer about *having* her near dogs. Later in the week, Java was asked to be a Demo Dog again. This time, she was asked to demonstrate the equipment she and I both knew like a broken-in pair of shoes. Since the first training with Edie

Jane, Java wore a Halti® head collar and step-in harness for almost every walk. I used a double-ended leash, with one end attached to the harness and the other end to the head collar, and used two hands to help maneuver her. These two points of contact allowed me to guide Java in changing or rebalancing her posture, and assisted in moving her head away or steering. And now, Java was given the chance to model her costume and show how effective it was to help an unbalanced dog make balanced choices.

A bit shy at first, Java walked hesitantly into the center of the circle of people and animals with Debby Potts as her leader. A few glances back at me to make sure it was all okay, then Java was off and performing. She showed flawlessly how easy it was for a reactive dog to feel balanced and confident with two simple pieces of equipment, and a leader who possessed an incredible amount of awareness and confidence. Like a flowing ballet, I watched Debby and Java stroll around the circle in a dance of balance, cooperation, focus, and love—passing other dogs, holding still, and moving slow.

Glancing around the circle, I was reaffirmed how much Java's spirit touched everyone else, as smiles and a few tears showed joy and gratitude. We closed out our second to last TTouch Training with joy, laughter, and feelings of accomplishment. I felt stronger and more balanced than I had at any other training, and Java seemed to be more centered as well. Packing up our stuff, Java and I said our goodbyes and thank yous. Kelly and I hugged our secret 'wagging tail' hug then talked on the phone to each other for most of the ride home. Java slept like a rock.

Java and I returned from our journey to find a happy man waiting for us in the driveway. With a big smile, open arms and a kiss, Allen was eager to take the leash, hear my stories, and hold me gently in his arms. It felt fabulous to be home. In only two short months of living together, being with Allen felt right, and I knew that just being near him was home. Allen knelt down to the hound by his side, held her muzzle up to his, and smiled.

"I missed you, Girlie!" he said, as he kissed Java quickly then tore around the yard with her.

Unloading the car, I watched with joy as the rest of my family was reunited with a play bow. Java and Allen followed me up the stairs to the cottage, as we opened the door to our colorful life. Panting and wagging, Java ran after Allen who headed to the kitchen to fix some fresh water for all of us. I followed behind, then put my arms around Allen's waist while he stood at the sink, and kissed the back of his soft neck.

"I'm really glad to be home," I whispered sweetly, as Allen turned around with a smile to hold me tighter.

"I'm glad to have you home," he replied with a kiss, then raced Java to the living room.

Java plunked herself down on the futon couch, then collapsed as much of her body as would fit onto Allen's lap. She was happy to be home, too. Using up what space was left, I curled up on the other side of Allen as he stretched his arm around me, then pulled me closer to his heart. Side by side we sat, sharing our dreams, and watching the huge, willow tree branches dance gracefully back and forth in the warm, summer breeze.

CHAPTER THIRTEEN

FAITH

"The wise heart is not one that understands everything. It is the heart that can tolerate the truth of not knowing."

~ Jack Kornfield

Faith rests patiently deep within our cells, waiting for golden opportunities to allow it to break free. When opportunities knock, we have a choice. Assuming we notice the opportunity in the first place, we can open the door, close the door, or stand frozen and do nothing. For some, those doors appear earlier in life. For others, they never seem to appear at all. And for many of us, we continue to enter the door within and thank our cells graciously for opening up to potential time and time again.

My faith is really strong, but sometimes I am overcome with doubting my own ability more than anything. With Java, I needed to continue to trust in myself, have faith, and let go in order to grant her the freedom she deserved. I wanted her to live a life that allowed her to cope better, relax more, and make wiser choices. That can be a tough thing to do when you have a dog who snarls and flails like a brown, hairy monster in a horror film.

Later that summer, an opportunity to improve the bond between Java and I appeared, and we accepted. Having built a new friendship with the owner of Top Dog Country Club, Jean and I talked of ways to trade TTouch work for her arthritic dog, Picasso, with something equally as valuable for Java. What was valuable for Java and I was the opportunity to have positive experiences with other dogs in safe environments.

It had been two years since Java's attack. Up until this point, she had been off leash around one new dog with a lot of supervision and fencing in between. Heading into a small, empty play yard at Top Dog, I felt my heart race as a large variety of dogs barked and wagged from the other side of the fence. Holding my breath, I found myself gripping

Java's leash tightly, then realized there was no reason for concern. Relaxing my death grip, I exhaled into calm. Java and I moved slowly toward the fence of dogs—one step at a time together—as I worked to help her with self-control. When we got about six feet away, I noticed Java's body start to tense, and watched her breathing shift from relaxed to shallow. She froze in fear, and I steered her away. Moving away, then closer, we took short breaks to regain our composure, then continued to walk back and forth in front of the fence at a great distance. I used the head collar to help steer Java's head away from a hard stare and potential outburst, and the harness on her body to help improve her balance and posture. As a strong back up, we perfected our 'Leave It' command just in case. Back and forth we walked—slowly, composed, breathing, trusting and balanced. The more we learned how to have faith in each other, the easier it was to dance with grace.

Java and I practiced on leash in this setting for a few visits, until finally, we were ready. Sometimes it takes trusting the baby steps in order to take a leap of faith. After trusting each other, Java and I showed signs of being more relaxed and confident around dogs, and we were both able to breathe, stand in balance, and watch without reacting. Trusting in myself and trusting in Java, I reached deep within and unclipped her leash.

Click.

Java looked up at me with surprise in her eyes and joy in her body. A huge smile on my face gave her the reassurance and permission she needed, as I watched her face shift to excitement. It felt like heaven to have her leash draped loosely around my neck, and see her without equipment on her body.

"Go on, Girlie. Run it out," I said joyously, waving my hand in the direction of the dogs.

With only a slight moment of hesitation, Java ran to the fence, and I exhaled. Java ran away, looked at me, ran back to the fence, barked a few times, then ran back for more. Turning toward me, she leaped through the air like a gazelle clicking her heels with pride, then ran around the play yard with joy. We had both worked hard to get to this point of making appropriate choices, and Java was ready to show me what she'd learned. Running back to check in with me, I stroked the length of Java's body and told her how proud I was of her. Then, she ran back to the fence to show off her true potential.

I watched in amazement as Java slowly approached a tan and white cocker spaniel from the side. Her body became tense and her breathing shifted, and for some reason, I felt ready to be disappointed. Java wouldn't allow it. She looked directly at the dog, curled her lip without ever making a sound, then lowered her lip back to its resting point. Turning swiftly, Java ran back to me to make sure I'd been paying attention.

What transpired in that millisecond was the foundation of Tellington TTouch® — how animals are able to change their habitual behavior through balancing mentally, physically and emotionally with a combination of TTouches and movements. What I witnessed was Java making a conscious choice not to *react*, but rather to engage her brain and make an appropriate choice to *act* instead. Tears of joy streamed down my cheeks, as Java bounced over to me with Plott Hound pride in her step. Singing songs of praise, I stroked the side of Java's body, then we celebrated our newfound freedom by playing with a tennis ball, and chasing each other through the kiddie pool.

Have you ever done something that set you free or set someone else free? Maybe it's as simple as choosing to say 'no' when society thought you should say 'yes'. Setting healthy boundaries can be a challenge, but once you learn to take control of your own life, it will set you free. When I finally had enough faith and trust to unclip the leash, a beautiful gift was returned from the trust I'd given Java that day.

Summer was filled with bike rides, bonfires, long walks, new romance, evolving romance and teaching Java that water wasn't scary. Java and I would often meet Allen for a picnic in the park after work then hop in his truck in search of the best ice cream in the suburbs. I looked forward to seeing him at the end of the day—to cook, dance, laugh, play guitar, cuddle, and share stories. It felt great to cook for two people and be able to touch, smell, and see Allen every day instead of only on the weekends. The downside of reality was that he worked full time and I was trying to get a new business going. We were both working far more than playing, and it took its toll on us both.

During late summer, Allen and I began to argue about little stuff. The kind of stuff where you're bugging each other, but you don't really know where it's coming from. No matter what, we weren't always nice to one another and neither one of us was sure why it was happening. It could've been the mosquitoes, hot, humid summer or continually bumping into each other in a 600 square foot cottage. It also could've been that we both got knocked off of our center when I moved in with him. My spirit felt squelched and it showed, and Allen seemed less centered and unhappy as well. We talked about finding a bigger, happier place to live, and Allen agreed that a winter cooped up in a tiny, cold cottage could be more trying than either one of us wanted
to try. Java agreed.

As summer came to a close, I forgot that as a former teacher I was supposed to have a three-month summer vacation. However, the place I chose to put myself in required me to promote or go broke. In no time at all, I had become part of the animal-care community, leaving the public teaching world behind, and I started to trade my services in order to learn more about other healing modalities. In return, Java and I were treated to many wonderful sessions.

As the fall leaves began to change color, Allen and I packed up our cottage, and moved about a mile away into a cute, yellow rental house with almost twice as much space. For the first time in her life, Java was able to experience a house with stairs, a fireplace, and wood floors. It felt fabulous to fix up our home together, and have what felt like a lot more space to cook, dance, share, create, and play. Along with the move, Allen and I forged an even deeper connection, and we were both happy to have created our first home together as a couple.

Two weeks after the move, Java and I headed to Cincinnati for our sixth and final TTouch Training. The founder of Tellington TTouch®, Linda Tellington-Jones, was the instructor for the week, and I was excited to meet her and have her get to know Java. I was looking forward to this session in particular because it was a familiar thread during a time which felt unfamiliar. I was grateful to spend time with people I knew, who also knew me. To split our travel time, Java and I treated ourselves to an overnight stay at a hotel in Chicago on our way to Cincinnati. Heading into the hotel with Java at my side, I smiled as we walked down the hall toward our room.

My mind drifted back to our first training with our first hotel only a year and a half before. I had been a scared woman with a scared dog, and now I felt more confident, balanced and relaxed. Unlocking the door to our room, Java bounded inside, then waited patiently for me to unclip her leash so she could explore her new space for the night. As I set down my backpack, I unclipped Java's leash, then glanced quickly at the large array of mirrors in the room. Memories of Java's violent display during our first hotel visit made me hope she wouldn't have a repeat performance. As old images of lunging and growling flooded my brain, I turned to see what choices Java would make *this* time.

Walking first into the bathroom, Java sniffed around while I watched with curiosity. Bouncing out of the bathroom, Java walked directly toward a full length mirror, stopped, turned her head to fully admire herself, then walked past her reflection. It was almost as if Java loved herself enough to stop and really notice the dog she'd become. The remainder of the night was spent watching cable and sleeping soundly together. It was pretty uneventful compared to our first hotel stay. I was glad. Java and I were in a fabulous place because we felt better about ourselves, and learned to like what we saw. I think we were becoming balanced.

Rolling into the Econo Lodge® for our last training was bittersweet. With Java sitting quietly in the back seat, I felt a sense of accomplishment and maturity rise from within myself. Kelly, Kathy, Judy and I were elated to see each other, and each time we got together for trainings they mentioned how much calmer and more balanced Java acted. We all changed and grew through this TTouch work as humans, too, and it was lovely to watch each of us unfold and blossom. Gathering in Judy's room the night before the training, we caught up on stories, and shared our plans after graduation. Then, we talked about what it would be like to meet Linda Tellington-Jones.

Java and I slept soundly together, then woke in time for a short walk to the motel lobby to grab a cup of coffee. In a year and a half's time, I had finally figured out a way to walk my reactive dog while carrying a hot cup of coffee—a short distance, nonetheless, but we did it.

Entering the training facility on Day One, I spotted a woman with short, blonde hair sporting a smile the size of the moon and a heart twice as big. With lemon yellow and Caribbean blue, silk scarves floating every which way, she walked over to Java and I with a warm smile, and even warmer heart.

"Hello, I'm Linda Tellington-Jones," she smiled into my eyes, and gave me a warm, gentle handshake.

"Who's this?" Linda asked, smiling down at Java who was looking directly back at her.

"This is Java," I smiled back, then exhaled and let the leash loosen in my hand.

Without so much as a fleeting moment passing, Linda bent over, cupped Java's velvety, brown, muzzle sweetly in her hands, then kissed her gently on her forehead.

"Hello, sweet Java girl!" Linda giggled as the two of them beamed love and acceptance back and forth.

Linda is a gifted woman. If anyone else had been that bold on a first meeting, they would have been startled with Java's lightning fast and not-always-so-pleasant reaction. However, Linda and Java shared a heart connection and understanding right away. What I love about Linda is how she accepts animals for who they are, and where they are, and that she loves them unconditionally right from the start. Animals sense an open heart.

Java seemed like a seasoned pro at our last training. She had better self-control during stressful situations, and her outbursts were less frequent and forceful. She was sleeping more, watching more, participating more, and reacting less. However, she also started to lunge and bark at people who were either not feeling well or were upset, which was a bit of a shift. It took awhile to pinpoint it, but she started to show me how some people exuded energy that was difficult for her to be around without reacting. She started to bark every time one of the teaching assistants got up, and it took a few days to realize it was the woman's red jacket that triggered Java's reaction. Strangely enough, once she turned her jacket inside out, Java didn't react anymore. Then, she started to back away from people who were sad, had headaches, or were grumpy.

At this session, I came to realize and understand Java's sensitivity to the world around her, and how much she covered up her fear by reacting. It was Linda's suggestions that helped us take the next huge steps in our journey, and truly look at our fears. Yep, we still had fears.

Still dressed in her TTouch costume (a dark green Full Body Wrap, tan Halti® head collar, and dark brown step-in harness), Java demonstrated a positive example of the true potential of a reactive dog. When Linda took the leash, I learned by watching, and sucked up knowledge like a sponge. Watching her whisper quietly to Java, Linda would point across the room to encourage Java to watch the other dogs calmly, instead of only looking away as she'd done in the past. Linda was teaching Java to face her fears, and in doing so, Java was able to see those fears dissolve before her eyes. Linda exhaled with Java, praised her, respected her, understood, loved, and trusted her. And I began to sincerely appreciate how lucky I was to find this career with Tellington TTouch® because it really *did* work.

By the third day, Linda was ready to nudge Java and I even further. Gently, of course.

"Does anyone have a neutral dog who would like to play with Java?" Linda clapped her hands together, then smiled to the group with her usual, upbeat enthusiasm.

Our TTouch group had been together for over a year and a half, and they'd all seen and heard Java's snarls and pearly whites more times than I'm sure they could count. There was dead silence to Linda's request, and my excitement turned quickly to embarrassment as I felt like the kid who was chosen last for dodge ball.

"I've been watching her, and this dog has absolutely no intention of harming. She just lacks confidence." Linda went on to clear the air, "If she never has the opportunity to make appropriate choices, she never will."

From the far side of the room came the sweet voice of an angel.

"Kita would *love* to play with Java," Kelly replied, then smiled at me. I could feel the rest of the room sigh in relief that the pressure was lifted.

"Wonderful! We'll take the two of them outside at the break so they can meet one another," Linda said to the group then looked down toward the Plott Hound at her side.

"Java, would you like to meet Kita?" she smiled brightly, as Java looked back to her with enthusiasm and trust.

You can only imagine how nervous I felt. Letting Java loose with another dog for the first time in two and a half years, in front of Linda Tellington-Jones, was not my idea of a good time, but I didn't know how lovely faith could be until I gave it a shot. At that time, Linda was somewhat of a complete stranger who trusted both Java and I, trusted herself, and felt certain it would all turn out perfectly. What makes Linda such a gem is how she takes animals (and humans) where they are in each moment without looking backward or forward.

Break time came quicker than I was prepared for, and the next thing I knew, Kelly was bouncing off the walls with Linda bouncing by her side. They thought this was fun! Both of them were giddy with excitement to take the dogs out to meet one another, while I stood nearby and hoped it would all turn out okay. They showed so much love and trust that my apprehension quickly melted into immense gratitude.

"Do you want me to put a basket muzzle on her?" I asked Linda hesitantly.

"Has she bitten?" she looked inquisitively at both Java and I, then smiled as if she were waiting for either one of us to respond.

"Never," I exhaled.

"Then, no," Linda responded firmly as she spun her body toward the door and waited for all of us to follow.

I didn't want to muzzle Java, but I also didn't know what would happen. Evidently, Linda did. We headed to the fenced yard in the back, with Kita the neutral dog, and an unmuzzled Java, the not-so-neutral dog. The space was large enough for both dogs to be let off leash about forty feet from each other. We unclipped the dogs' leashes at the door, then let them into the space one at a time. Kita walked far away from Java to give her space, then began sniffing the ground.

Java stood next to Linda, Kelly and I, sniffed the ground, and paid little attention to Kita. A few wags, sniffs from a distance, and a lot of encouragement from the humans to get the dogs to play, left us standing in amazement as Kita and Java wandered around calmly. Leashing up the dogs, we went inside to report to the group about the beautiful and uneventful meeting. My colleagues were astounded, and I felt unbelievably proud of Java and myself. Furthermore, I had a great appreciation for Linda, Kelly and Kita for giving Java and I the opportunity to succeed. It was a milestone for all of us because Java had experienced a positive interaction with another dog. Success had occurred on many levels. I trusted Linda and Kelly's knowledge and Kita's dog skills, and they trusted that Java was ready to make smart choices. Me, I finally trusted both Java and myself.

Journal Entry
10/18/03 – TTouch Training: Graduation Day

Java is wearing only a head collar and a fleece coat. She's been able to make better choices and keep herself calmer, and she doesn't seem to need her Full Body Wrap and harness anymore. When she reacts, Linda walks her into the circle to show her that nothing's going to get her and that it's not scary. She's making choices to go closer to dogs and people on her own, and has made incredible progress this week. Java is lying down calmly, facing the circle, and she's watching another dog being worked on by Linda only ten feet away. She shared direct eye contact with a dog only five feet from her and chose to blink and look away on her own! It's amazing to me how far we've come in such a short time.

By the end of the week, Java walked repeatedly into the circle on her own, then back to me for praise and reassurance. She chose to walk closer to dogs and people, and made immense progress in a short while. For the first time in all six trainings, she was lying down, facing the circle, and watching the other dogs calmly and curiously from about ten feet away. I felt better about myself than I had in a long time, and was excited to graduate from the TTouch program so I could focus on Dancing Porcupine full time.

Java and I graduated from the TTouch Training on October 18, 2003, and I became a Certified Tellington TTouch Practitioner for Companion Animals. To mark our accomplishments, Allen welcomed home his two girls with a congratulatory banner stretched across our entire dining room wall, and a medal of honor to hang around my neck. It was a wonderful homecoming, and I started to feel like our new home was helping us create more balance.

Allen and I often sat by the fire together, telling stories or lying quietly in silence. Sometimes, Java, Allen, and I would sit on the couch to watch a movie or wait for some form of wildlife to come into our front yard. Even though we were in a small suburb, we were given the gift of an occasional red fox, white-tailed deer, or raccoon in front of the huge picture window. It seemed we were just beginning to figure things out together as a couple, but we were both exhausted from trying to figure things out at all.

As winter approached, so did depression and anxiety, and I found myself feeling like something was missing. I longed for the calm, centered man I'd fallen in love with, and the beautiful, strong, resilient women I'd forgotten along the way. Depression sucks. There's no two ways around it.

If you can get inside of depression, it's only an opportunity for growth that's been covered up with a wet, soggy, blanket. What I realized about depression was that the blanket could be lifted if you sat still, acknowledged it, accepted it, and then let it go. My depression came and went as I worked hard to figure out my own stuff, while Allen worked hard to figure out why his stuff wasn't merging with mine. When you still carry baggage, it can be very heavy. The blessing that existed between Allen and I was that we both loved each other immensely and worked our tails off to try to create more peace and harmony in our relationship. What we neglected to realize was that we both lost parts of ourselves in the process. Once you lose your individuality, it's difficult to be in a healthy relationship.

Neither one of us was as happy or centered as when we dated long distance, and we found ourselves struggling to keep the peace. It felt like hanging onto a cliff and having a bunch of tiny little rocks slipping out from underneath your fingers, and we both wondered if the big rock was going to fall, yet hoped it wouldn't.

As Allen and I struggled to live together without losing ourselves, I struggled to find more friends and feel like I fit into my new life. I was starting to worry about money and wondered if moving to Minnesota had been a smart decision. Deep down I knew that following my heart was the right decision, but my mind began to race as my savings started to decrease. As the intensity in our relationship began to increase, Allen and I knew we needed to work harder on our relationship and ourselves, but we didn't have the skills to make it happen. Our communication had broken down to a place of misunderstandings and hurt feelings, and as more rocks began to fall, I began to put more energy into the only thing that felt comfortable—working with animals.

Within two months of graduating from my TTouch program I taught half-day workshops, and after three months, I published my first article in a local Twin Cities newspaper *(Twin Cities Wellness/Essential Wellness)*. Within six months, I published my second article in *Twin Cities Dog Magazine*, and by summer, I was flown to Toledo, Ohio to speak about Tellington TTouch® at the International Association of Animal Massage and Bodyworkers Conference. My private clients were picking up and my workshops were filling up, but Allen and I were sadly wondering if we were better off being split up. Java continued to grow, and with a few new friends who trusted both of us, we were able to find two canine playmates for Java. A few trips to a secluded dog park at the wee hours of the morning showed me the beauty of letting go, having faith, and watching my deprived hunting dog chase a deer through the woods.

Splashing through streams and getting muddier than ever, we began to enjoy the outdoors off leash, again. For added security and less stress for both of us, Java and I moved our playtime to a fully fenced baseball diamond. Java fell madly in love. A two-year-old boxer/pit mix, Lewis stole Java's heart the moment she laid eyes on him. Well, right after she tried to kick his butt.

As much as my friend Trisha and I had created a foolproof plan to introduce Lewis to Java, we didn't plan quite well enough for the Plott Hound-sized hole in the fence. With Java running free inside the fenced baseball diamond, Trisha leashed Lewis and brought him up to the fence so the two dogs could sniff, but Java wanted a closer look. She barked, jumped, wagged her tail and made a beeline for the six-inch opening in the gate. Then, she went after Lewis. Java sniffed, snarled, snapped and carried on, while Lewis snarled back and the noise festival began.

With what seemed like an eternity, Trisha held Lewis' leash loosely, watching the two dogs calmly, while I watched nearby in amazement. Time slows when dogs snarl. In reality, it was no more than three seconds, but three seconds seems like a lifetime when you see a whole bunch of slobber, pearly whites, and hear snarly, snappy noises coming from two big dogs. Then, they stopped.

Standing patiently, Java and Lewis waited for directions from their humans while the humans stood and stared at one another.

"I need to either get her inside the fence or take her home," I told Trisha nervously—concerned that Java would run off.

"I think they're done," Trisha laughed as she looked down at the two calm dogs by her side. "I brought two beers in my backpack, so I say let's go in," she replied with a smile.

Trisha explained how she had watched Java and Lewis the entire time they were snarling, and neither one of them had any intention of harming the other. It was a jam session with a lot of noise and slobber. From then on, the two lovebirds ran and played frequently. What a great feeling to watch Java run free with another dog—to watch her initiate play, roll in the muddy grass, and come running back with floppy ears, a big mouthful of drool, and a huge smile of gratitude.

During this time that my business was flourishing and Java's issues were decreasing, the bottom continued to slip between Allen and I. It made me unbelievably sad and angry, and I started to vent my anger and cry more than I ever expressed in my life. I felt suicidal, depressed, anxious, confused and out of sorts for what seemed like most of the summer. It was 'Dark Night of the Soul' kind of stuff where you feel like you're being sliced, diced and julienned. Inner work, I think that's what it's called. Well, it sucks. As hard as he tried, Allen didn't know what to do to help. I was losing him while

I was losing myself, and Allen was losing himself while he was losing me. We spent a lot of time and energy trying to understand one another—wrapped in each other's arms, wiping tears from our eyes and each other's cheeks, arguing, running away, and running closer. What it felt like to me was trying to hang on tight to something that was slippery. Even though you knew it would slip eventually, you hung on anyway because you never wanted to let it go. When you're crazy in love with someone, you do that sort of thing.

By summer's end, I was enjoying public speaking engagements and my business, Dancing Porcupine, was gaining more notoriety. Java and I were able to enjoy short walks together, and people often stopped us on the street to ask her breed or remark at how well trained she was. Java started to make better choices when she saw other dogs, and I continued to become more aware of how aware I needed to be in all of my relationships.

Journal Entry
8/30/04 - Calm

Today was the first day ever that Java didn't snarl at the broom. I'm amazed at how calm she's becoming—so much less reactive to everything. We've also made incredible progress with nail trimming by using the TTouch Body Wrap, Python Lifts, and Raccoon TTouches before we trim. That's been a really long road since an unpleasant grooming experience at a pet store as a puppy. She played with four little kids in the yard last week but still lunges at some adults once in awhile if they lean over or reach toward her.

She still needs time to decompress in new situations and I realize her stress levels (and mine) so much more. She never used to approach people at all and now she will but lunges if they try to touch her right away. I need to pay better attention myself, and to train the humans more quickly. Java does great when people let her sniff and come to them. She senses fear easily and needs a little extra time and space to figure people out. So do I.

Journal Entry
9/4/04 - Success

Today was the first day ever that Java fell sound asleep outside.

At the end of September, I headed to Denver, Colorado to the Association of Pet Dog Trainer's Conference to learn more from the experts. Almost a year passed since my TTouch graduation and I itched to learn more about animals. What stuck out during these four days was how I was actually doing a great job of working with animals. Most of what I learned, I learned by doing, trying, making mistakes, and doing over. Listening to Patricia McConnell, Marc Bekoff, and Turid Rugaas speak at the conference, I felt proud of myself. Intuitively, I had made some great choices for Java over the years and it felt great to have validation from the experts.

I was becoming an expert myself, and I hadn't even realized it. I had cut back on things she couldn't cope with, like being left alone in the car or long walks, and I also decreased her stress levels by changing her to a low protein diet and reducing forced exercise. Java and I spent a lot of time sitting still to learn what sitting still felt like, and we laughed, played hide-and- seek, and did what felt right.

I wasn't one who learned everything from schooling, but rather learned from having Java as a companion—trying to find ways to make both our lives more manageable and pleasurable. Plus, I learned from all the other challenging animals I was blessed to work with. What I wasn't able to find a solution for, was how to work with challenging humans, which included myself.

As much as I continued to feel better about my business, I felt worse about myself, and my relationship with Allen. Neither one of us was treating the other with the same loving kindness that brought us together, and I felt like it was only a matter of time before one, or both of us, mustered up the strength to change our situation. It didn't seem like anyone in our house was very happy.

I wondered what my purpose was supposed to be—why I chose to leave everything comfortable to live in a place of discomfort and uncertainty. I felt myself spiraling to a place that seemed all too familiar—a place I'd been near the end of my marriage five years before. Alone. I'd already walked away once from someone I loved in order to save myself, and this time I wasn't too eager to repeat the same pattern of being the one to leave.

Call it wisdom or stupidity, but I hung in there, stood still, and waited for something to change. Two months later, it did.

CHAPTER FOURTEEN

LETTING GO

"The brook would lose its song if you removed all the rocks."

~ American Proverb

My rock moved out. Actually, it was more like an avalanche that I intuitively knew was coming but never believed it would sideswipe so suddenly. Allen and I had been together about two years, and in one day, we were apart. I was filled with extreme sadness and unbelievable rage, but soon realized I could only be angry with myself.

It stinks when you're mad at yourself. All of my choices were my own, but now that *he* made a choice that was healthy for *him*, I didn't like it. It was also healthy for me, but it took a few more days to realize it. I felt like a crazy woman, filled with emotion, ready to go into the ring and duke it out. I felt betrayed, deceived, sad, angry, scared, and somewhat relieved.

If you've ever been through passionate extremes in a relationship, you understand how fire can ignite seductively, roar passionately, and dwindle slowly. Allen and I had been madly in love with each other, but lost ourselves in the process.

With a part time job, a new business, and my financial support moving *his* plants and furniture out of our house this time, I knew I needed to find peace within myself to forgive, let go and move on. Easier said than done. Once again, I found myself lying on the couch with Java nestled warmly by my side, and I cried. I cried for the times that were, and the times that would never be. I cried, cried, and cried some more, and felt sorry for myself for days, but something inside me had changed since the last time I'd been alone. This time, I wasn't afraid. Lying on the couch with my arm around my hound, I realized how far we'd come, and how much courage it took us to get where we were.

Strength. Perseverance. Resiliency.

I'm sure there have been times in your life where you needed to dig as deep as you could. Think back to a time when you needed to find the strength to move forward, yet you felt paralyzed and stayed in the moment because it was easier. Sometimes I become paralyzed when I have challenges, but usually only for a short while. Now I was faced with a big challenge and I knew I couldn't sit still for long.

I knew the Universe had a plan for me, but I didn't want to go without Allen. When two people love one another, and they can't figure out how to be themselves enough to stay together, it's pretty painful. I've been in love enough times to know how it feels to walk away from it—or have someone else walk away. I probably have a bump on my forehead from slapping my hand there so many times.

With Allen, I needed to let go and trust that the Universe knew what was right. Allen needed time and space to learn how to take care of himself and become whole again. I needed to remember how I was supposed to do the same. Living alone is a great incubator for self-love. I'm a typical Cancer, so letting go is a lesson that keeps popping up and saying an ugly hello to me.

Some days I'd like to punch old 'Letting Go' in the nose and make it go away for good. Although it's a challenge for me to let go, I'm grateful for the opportunities to continue to practice. Some people are able to quickly let go like a puff of smoke that takes their troubles away in an instant.

Me, I like to hang on with my talons and slowly let go one nail at a time—making sure there's a lot of energy involved. It's much more painful, drawn out, and dramatic that way. That's another thing Java, has taught me. Letting go is a process, and that it's okay to be *who* you are and *where* you are.

I fought desperately to let go of my strong heart connection with Allen because I didn't want to believe that parts of the magic we created changed dramatically after I chose to move to Minnesota. I loved him more than anyone I'd ever loved, yet I also felt more loneliness, anger, and sadness than ever before. On the upside, I also felt an immense amount of love, kindness, tenderness, and support throughout our relationship, and I knew if anything positive would come of it, I needed to pull up my bootstraps and change, too. Resiliency was asking me if I wanted to play.

What does it mean to be resilient? Think about the times in your life where something seemed like a big challenge. Maybe it's as simple as how to carry three bags of groceries, and a lamp, with two hands. Or maybe it's something bigger like losing your job or facing a challenge in a relationship. No matter how big or small the problem, you always have a choice—focus on the problem, or focus on the solution. When we give energy to a problem, it becomes more of a problem. If we give our energy toward trying to find a solution, the problem seems to fade away.

Bless my family for being the ones to kick me in the butt whether I want them to or not. My sister helped me to erase financial fears by talking me through reality, and my mom listened compassionately to my roller coaster of emotions. After the initial anger and sadness cloud dissipated, I realized Allen wasn't gone forever, and that he truly *was* a good guy.

However, I found myself in a bit of a predicament. I was without full time work and couldn't afford to live in the house that Allen and I rented together. Shifting into survival zone, I let go of the emotion that consumed me in order to reserve my energy to take care of Java and I. It was the beginning of winter, and I found myself lying in front of the fireplace and staring at the shadows that danced across the ceiling. I'd been here before—right after my marriage dissolved—and I wondered why I was revisiting a familiar place in my life.

What did I do wrong?
What did I do right?
What the hell was I going to do now!?

Anger helps to let go, but sadness sure doesn't. What I needed to let go of was the dream of being with the same person forever—living a life of peace and harmony with another being for eternity. I wasn't there yet.

As I laid in front of the fire, thoughts drifted through my consciousness, and my breathing slowed to a shallow pace. Java walked into the room and stood over my head with her hot breath breathing into mine. Tears rolled off my cheeks, then onto the floor, as Java watched them fall.

"I'm glad I have you," I whispered to Java.

Java stood over me with her ears flopped forward, and looked into my green amber eyes with her chestnut browns. Licking my nose with vigor, she ran to get a toy while I smiled at what a happy dog she was. Dropping a half-torn, squeakerless cow, Java waited patiently for me to engage. Play is a wonderful way to remember how to open your heart.

The house seemed empty but familiar—eerily similar to how it felt when Java and I lived alone after Clio died, but the difference now was that I felt stronger and wiser. A few weeks passed and I worried, wondered, and started to take much better care of myself. I was eating better, sleeping better, and slipping easily back into my morning yoga routine. Somewhere along my journey, I had forgotten myself, what I loved and who I was. When you live alone, you learn to remember yourself.

As I headed to my neglected yoga space in the basement, Java followed lazily down the steps. Sitting down with my legs stretched in front of me, I reached for my toes and exhaled. Java crawled across the floor on her belly, then flopped over on her side, wagged her tail, and looked over at me. Continuing on, my mind, body, and spirit became one as thoughts of 'hanging on' weighed themselves against 'letting go'. I felt heavy inside from hanging on and wanted to become free inside, and in one special moment during my downward dog yoga pose, I let go and forgave Allen. *POOF!* Just like healthy people do.

A graceful transformation of the heart occurred, and it allowed me to physically feel my heart release, let go, and become free from resentment. When you forgive completely, you're able to let go of holding onto 'what was' and wishing for 'what might be.'

My Grandma Fern used to say, "You can wish in one hand, and spit in the other, and see what you get the most of."

Patooey!

CHAPTER FIFTEEN

FREEDOM

"Freedom's just another word for nothing left to lose."

~ Kris Kristofferson

With nothing left to lose, and everything to gain, I took my life by the horns, and kicked my own self in the rear. In just two year's time I had dissolved an immense amount of fear for a chance at mutual love, and it happened completely. Love caressed my soul in the most beautiful and gentle way imaginable, and I had received absolutely everything I asked for, and then some. By believing in myself, I had found a way to make money petting animals, and had experienced mutual love with a man who loved Java as much as he loved me.

You know though, it's hard to get rid of the ugly thing called desire, but that's what sets us free—letting go of desire and expectation. I wanted to be free inside—free from the dark emotions I allowed to have control over me for such a long time—freedom to love unconditionally and wholeheartedly. I wanted to be free from suffering so I could roll like a big, fat, happy pig in a huge pile of love.

After I forgave Allen, there was an even tougher task. I needed to forgive myself. For some time, I beat myself up for thinking I made the wrong choice, at the wrong time, with the wrong guy. Looking back, none of it was wrong. In actuality, it was all a beautiful web filled with tiny amethyst gemstones, and a few pebbles that I hadn't acknowledged as glorious yet.

As I worried and wondered myself into a whirlwind of emotion, I came to the realization that everything happens as it's supposed to. I was the luckiest woman in the Universe to have lived such a rich life already, so I quit whining, counted my blessings, and took action for my own life.

Freedom is asking for help, then allowing the Universe to respond. So, within a few weeks of realizing I needed to find a new place to live, I asked. Lying in bed one night, I prayed for a small home with a fenced yard—reciting almost the same prayer I said the day I left my ex-husband. This time, what had changed was my ability to reach out and ask for help, and I did. I sent notes to my friends, family, and colleagues asking if they would please pray not only for a small house with a fenced yard (in a safe neighborhood), but also to add a prayer for Allen. When you truly come to a place of unconditional love, you want the best for others, too.

Within a month's time, Java and I were able to buy a perfect house for ourselves in Saint Paul, Minnesota. When I say we both bought it, we did. Without her input, I wouldn't have ever considered 'sunshine' as being the most important thing in buying a home. I finally asked her advice after searching and searching, and that's what she told me—sunshine. Isn't it beautiful to live in a way that makes sunshine the most important characteristic in buying a home?

Java and I found everything we were looking for, and more. This time, I was blessed with a large group of friends to help move my stuff into the crooked, old house that was all mine. By some miraculous feat, Allen and I continued to communicate positively, and he worked really hard to make my move as pleasurable as possible. Sure, there were a ton of emotions flying around my heart, but I wanted to find a way to keep him in my life in some way, too. He felt the same. In two year's time, Allen and I had become best friends that were unable to live together in harmony. Yet from moving apart, it allowed both Allen and I to find it in our hearts to become more aware and healthier for ourselves and each other. We changed, learned and continued to grow individually into separate, whole beings who still cared a lot for one another, and for Java. As my truckload of stuff pulled up to my new, single girl house, Allen was there to make sure the fenced yard was repaired for Java.

How did Java fare with all of this change? Overall, she did great. It's incredible to me how adaptable she is. In no time flat she found her 'spot' in the house, perched atop the bed in a perfect lookout position to make sure the entire neighborhood was keeping in line. With a fenced yard, I soon discovered the difference in her barks, and how the higher pitched ones were signals of her level of fear. She'd often come running to the door with wide eyes for me to let her inside quickly, please. It used to be that she jumped six feet in the air with every limb going a different direction, so scurrying quickly, and keeping all four feet on the ground, is a huge improvement. My new screen door appreciates her maturity as well.

Java and I snuggled under the covers in our new house and watched single girl movies like we had during our first two years together. I also spent more time taking her running, walking, and doing TTouch work with her. The biggest challenge with the move became her inability to act appropriately when new people came to the house. In the past, she kept her distance and barked—afraid to approach someone new, but this shifted into a new behavior that was sometimes difficult to predict.

Java was now able to keep her feet on the ground, but would run up to new people at the door before she was calm enough to make a smart choice. If the person reached out to touch this exuberant hound (which most people do), she would jump and snap at them because she was uncertain, or afraid. When animals are in a stressful state, their brains disengage. The same is true with humans.

It only took a few of Java's lunges for me to notice that she needed help when she met new people, but at least I was learning. When strangers came over, I leashed Java and often gave her something fabulous to chew on. The mouth is the connection to learning and emotion, so giving a dog something to chew when they are in a stressful state allows them to calm down. Sometimes I'd put Java outside with a bone or in a different room depending on who was coming to the house. If I wasn't able to give my attention to Java, I made it easier for everyone involved by removing her. In order to make our lives less stressful, I trained the humans walking in the door instead of expecting that Java would always make the best choice. When old friends stopped by, she remembered and it was simple. When Allen stopped by for a visit, I watched the two of them roll around on the floor, play, and laugh together like old times.

Living alone, I began to fall in love with myself all over again. I kept myself busy by decorating and painting my new home, promoting my business, taking better care of myself, and building an even stronger bond with Java. I forgot how much time we used to spend each day playing hide-and-seek and hunting games, teaching, learning, and welcoming the silence. I'd also forgotten how much I loved doing the same with children, and wondered if there was a way I could work with kids and animals together.

As I pictured my life the way I wanted it to be, what I saw for the first time was a stunning picture of myself as both a schoolteacher and animal trainer. Within the last ten years, I had developed a unique ability to bring out the true potential in both kids and animals. I had always seen myself in dual roles before—first as teacher, next as animal trainer—and secretly wondered if there was a way to integrate them both into a career to fulfill my dream.

Sometimes we might have a dream that's best left alone, but I prayed this wasn't the case. I really wanted to find a way at some point in my life to use my work with animals to connect with children of all ages. I wasn't really sure what that meant, or what form that may take, so I asked the Universe to show me how I could best serve. My faith is really strong, and I believe the Universe always has a plan.

The Universe had an awesome plan for me. After three months of wondering whether my purpose was solely to make money by petting animals, I received my first phone call for an interview. I had applied for a job that literally popped out of the classified section in the newspaper, and jumped into my heart. I had a decision to make, and it was time to listen to what the Universe had to offer. This particular job was one of the many I had applied for, but one of the few I was truly interested in. I wasn't willing to settle. Checking in with how my body felt was vital for me, so when the call came in, I was excited. That's a good sign.

Face to Face Academy is a charter high school on Saint Paul's east side. The school focuses on working with students with challenges, by providing them with an education that fits their needs. That pretty much means that the kids have issues that aren't being addressed completely in public schools and they need help. They're the misunderstood porcupines. Just the kind I like!

I accepted the interview for the following week, then looked in my closet. Animal trainer clothes filled up most of the space between the few pairs of dress pants and silk blouses. Over the course of two years, I had rearranged my wardrobe to suit my career, and now I had an interview.

Did I want to dress up for work every day? Not really.

The day of the interview, I dug in my closet and resurrected a pair of grey dress pants with a tiny lavender pinstripe, a black sleeveless sweater, and a lavender silk jacket. As I drove to the interview, I did a lot of thinking and feeling.

Was this an opportunity to fulfill my dream of working with kids and animals together?

If TTouch can help challenging animals, can it also help challenging teenagers?

Would I still be able to keep Dancing Porcupine?

My belly felt fine the entire seven-minute drive to the school, and when I entered the building, I felt even better. Soft, calm energy filled the spaces between the classical music and wicker chairs. Sitting down, I adjusted my fancy outfit, then waited for the first interview I'd had in eleven years.

A tall, lean, grey-haired man came out to greet me as a look of wonder filled my body. His gentle eyes put me more at ease as he outstretched his warm hand to shake mine.

"Hi, I'm Jim. I'm the Director of Face to Face Academy," he smiled as we shook hands, then walked out of the lobby. "We're going to head into the Academy on the other side of the building," he said, then motioned for me to follow.

I followed close behind, then stopped and smiled. Greeting us through the window on the other side of the Academy door was an apricot-colored standard poodle. I could hardly contain myself.

"Wow! Whose dog?" I blurted out like a five-year-old opening a birthday present.

"Oh, that's Royal. She's mine. She comes to school with me a few times a week. You could probably teach me a few things about her," Jim smiled, as we entered his comfortable, homey office.

I smiled with gratitude as I realized the near perfect nature of this meeting. It was a gem of an opportunity for me to work with challenging kids, and also use the knowledge I had gathered from working with challenging animals. The power of intention is with us at every turn.

The moment I sat down, I felt like I was in a friend's living room. Jim was wearing a pair of blue jeans and dark blue, cable knit sweater. I felt overdressed. We talked casually, and I laughed as I told him how I had dug out my 'real clothes' for the interview. With a warm chuckle back, he informed me that I indeed could have worn my khaki cargo pants, orange sweater, and orange boots to the interview. My mind flipped the pages of my past as a question about my future presented itself.

Did I want to work with challenging teenagers?
Did I even know how?

For nine years, I had worked as an art instructor with young children, leaving my position because it was no longer challenging. When Java came into my life, I began my journey of working with challenging animals, but something had been missing. My dream was to work with animals and kids together, and now, here was an opportunity that brought me closer to that dream.

Should I leap?

I accepted a full time Education Assistant position at Face to Face Academy a week later—a position that would be temporary and possibly shift to part time in two months. For a brief moment, I wondered what might happen in two months, but then realized the power of letting go. Whatever was supposed to happen, would happen. What an Education Assistant position in a small school meant to a former public schoolteacher like myself is very little teaching, very little grading, and no curriculum design. It also meant I'd be able to interact with kids again, and make a difference in somebody's life each day.

Making a difference matters to me, whether it's me making the difference with an animal or human, or another creature making a difference in my life. With this teaching job, I knew I'd still be able to schedule private sessions and teach workshops with Dancing Porcupine, and I'd also have medical and dental benefits which is very exciting for someone who's made their living as a sole proprietor for a couple of years. I could pay my bills without worrying, and be close enough to my house that I could run home to let Java out at lunchtime if I wanted to. I wanted to.

It didn't take long for me to realize I was sharing my knowledge with shy and reactive teenagers, and shy and reactive animals. Funny how that works. I applied what I already knew was successful with animals, and within a short time, felt accepted by the students. Many of them were eager to learn more about my animal work and to try out those 'weird', 'cool' or 'stupid' circular TTouches on their own arms or legs. I learned that in order to work with reactive kids, I needed to help them find their balance just as I did with the animals—mentally, physically and emotionally.

Within the first two months I worked hard to find ways to encourage and respect the students, and help build their self-esteem and confidence. I also mixed in heavy doses of love, trust and understanding. As the school year came to a close, Dancing Porcupine was still flourishing strongly. My position at the school would be shifting from full time to part time, so I had another big decision to make.

Was it possible to manifest more?

I loved the life I had created. I was working with both kids and animals, and I intended to continue it. At the same time, I let go to the fact that I had asked the Universe to guide me along the path I was meant to follow. My job was to surrender, be patient, and accept the help that was given.

What was handed to me next was a closer step toward my dream should I wish to take it. It seemed the school was desperately in search of a licensed art teacher to round out their program. The position would require me to work with challenging kids thirty hours a week, which would allow me the freedom to continue working with challenging animals as well. There's nothing that fires me up more than the freedom of loving what you do, and doing what you love.

Bring it on!

CHAPTER SIXTEEN

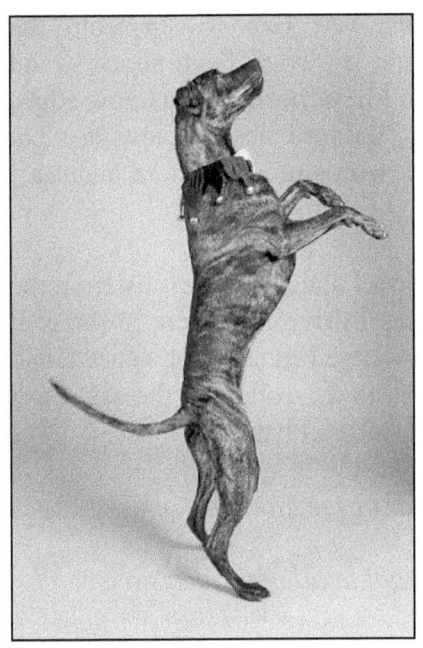

BALANCE

"Balance lies in knowing what needs rest."

~ *Source Unknown*

Sometimes I sit back, watch the threads of my life stitch together, and smile. I'm really blessed. As I page through my past, I see the mysterious web I've woven from the opportunities that have come my way. Each silver strand gently embraces the woman I have been, and acknowledges the woman I have become. Balance lies in knowing what needs rest, and those seven words are a personal mantra I chant daily.

A small beaded medicine wheel dangles gracefully from the rearview mirror in my car as I drive from here to there. It reminds me on a daily basis where I'm feeling balanced, and where I'm lacking. As I look to the yellow in the east I ask myself how I'm doing with spiritual balance.

Am I spending time in prayer or meditation?

Am I moving closer to the light in all of my decisions?

I wait patiently for the answers to rest in my knowing before moving on. With a brief pause, I acknowledge, then look toward the red in the south as I check in truthfully with my emotional being.

Am I holding on to anything I need to let go of?

How does my heart feel? My belly?

Again, I wait for the answers to find themselves within before I continue. To the black in the west, I check my physical body.

Am I eating well, and getting enough rest?

Am I practicing yoga, walking, or finding other ways to engage my body?

Waiting patiently, the answers appear. Moving on to the white in the north I remind myself to take care of my mind and thoughts.

Am I spending enough time quieting my whole being?

Am I enjoying stillness of body and mind?

My ritual comes to a close each morning as I gently rub the beads in the center of the cross where the four directions come together. It is one last reminder as to where I need to put my energy for the day. Dogs just shake their bodies to do the same thing.

As I drive to work each day, I listen to people like Caroline Myss, Carlos Castañeda, don Miguel Ruiz, Shakti Gawain, and Byron Katie on my CD player. They remind me what's important, but no matter whom I listen to, whether it is myself or someone else, the same message comes through. Trust your inner self and do your own inner work. We have only ourselves in this lifetime, and what a gift we can give when we open our heart to all that comes our way. The students at Face to Face remind me daily how important it is to love unconditionally, be nonjudgmental, respectful, and to love all creatures.

It's the weekend now as I write our final chapter. This morning, Java and I took another leap together, and danced our way into the woods. We haven't done that in a long time—really pushed ourselves to grow as a team. Sometimes I still find that I need a nudge to go to that next level with Java, otherwise I sit in a place that's comfortable and easy, and we never grow. I'm not much different than anyone else with a challenging dog. I still worry, wonder, hope, and give myself a lot of pep talks before I embark on a new adventure. I also check carefully to make sure that Java will be safe, and so will any other animals. Although I can't always predict what will happen, what I know now is that if I don't give her the opportunity to grow, she never will—and neither will I.

With a short lecture on keeping her teeth in her mouth, Java and I headed to a large, wooded dog park not far from my house just as the sun was coming up. As I reminded myself to breathe, Java bounded out of the car, then bounced toward the entryway with exuberance. Looking around at the barren park, I didn't notice any dogs in sight. A part of me felt disappointed, yet another part felt relieved.

As I watched Java sniff and leave her urine business card on the pile of wood chips where well-adjusted dogs play, we continued on toward the wooded trails. As I looked up the hill, I watched a person and a dog engaging in play near the edge of the tall grasses. A combination of fear and excitement filled my chest as I followed Java to a large clearing in the woods. I watched closely as a brown and white hound came barreling down the hill, while Java pushed her nose deeply into the tall grasses to sniff the fresh earth.

A woman waved from atop the hill, and as her hound came flying down the slope toward mine, I asked if he was good with other dogs. That's one thing I definitely know about Java—that she does *great* with male dogs who understand dog language. Dissolving some of my anxiety, the woman was unconcerned when I told her that Java may snarl at her dog—or she may not.

"Java, pay attention. There's a pup coming," I said slowly and easily to her. Then I exhaled, let go of my fears, and watched.

Java looked up, looked around, missed seeing the dog completely, then ran straight up the hill at top speed to find the canine I was referring to. By the time she finally noticed, the dog was at my feet. Java raced down the hill, slowed at the bottom, then began a game of chase with the hound. A few slight air snaps of her mouth reminded me to stay calm, talk with her, and guide her. As I watched her run with all four feet on the ground, I smiled as she tried to herd the lazy hound dog away from me. We're still working on some things.

Finally, both dogs came to a halt, and the true test was on. Java sniffed. He sniffed. Java made some sort of half-hearted, habitual vocalization, then the two dogs ran and chased one another. Within five minutes, Java was loping playfully through the woods, and wagging her tail loosely with joy. Periodically, she'd come back to check in and receive her praise in treats and smiles, then she was off— down the trail, sniffing, panting, and leaping tall grasses with her hunting dog buddy. We only stayed for about twenty minutes, but there has been nothing more glorious in our journey thus far as watching Java as she initiated play with a bow.

I try to get Java around new dogs about once a month in a variety of situations. Sometimes it's just on our walks, but other times it might be during off-peak hours at the dog park, or while she's running free in the baseball diamond with her boyfriend, Lewis. In between, we both need time to process and rest, so we don't overdo it. The resting time allows Java's adrenaline to go back to a normal level before it spikes up again. Mine, too.

It was almost a year since our last time at a dog park, and I held off with the hope we'd both become more balanced and able to be around other dogs without wetting our pants, or peeing on bushes every twelve seconds. With regular runs with Lewis, I felt like backing off was a smart thing to do—

to get both of us to a place where we felt calm and comfortable around one dog before introducing her to others. I'm glad we've gone forward slowly because we've experienced a lot of success together.

In the time we've been percolating, I continue to do TTouch work with Java. I use Python Lifts and a Body Wrap to help with nail trimming, and use circular TTouches to decrease stress for vet visits. I use a variety of TTouches on her entire body daily just to help her remember who and where she is. Ear TTouches are her favorite by far, and she often lowers her head now to get frequent head rubs. We also spend time working with the Playground for Higher Learning, and taking time to engage all of her senses when we go for slow walks on garbage day. Java reminds me how to touch her, where, how lightly, how much, or how little. She still reminds others sometimes, but we're working on fine tuning some things.

Our walks have become much more enjoyable and playful, and as I look down the relaxed leash these days, I see a dog who's calm, quiet, and balanced. When I follow the leash up from Java to my hand, I see a woman who mirrors her dog. In the past five years, Java and I have learned to enjoy ourselves and each other more, cope with stress better, and relax into the world that surrounds us.

I've seen so much change transpire since our paths crossed five years ago. Java now lies quietly much of the time when she looks out the window, rather than lunging and barking at the glass. The blinds can stay open, and I actually have furniture in front of the windows. She's able to lie quietly in a separate room, and even stays put when I get up and walk around the house. She's no longer crated when I'm gone, and handles herself perfectly at home. Sure, she still barks at the mailman, and at dogs and cats that are right in front of our house, but she's come so far that the big things have become little, and they don't matter as much to me anymore. Java used to pant obsessively and stare out the window with slobber falling from her mouth just waiting for my return from the mailbox, so we've come a long way!

Her beautiful eyes have softened from experience, and now I see more brown than white. The white shows up once in awhile as a reminder that there's still more for us to learn, but what we've learned already is enough for now. Just the other day, I smiled at the thought that every day is a positive day for Java and I, whereas in the past, she drove me nuts (and vice versa) five out of seven days in the week.

Java's much more independent, and plays much more than she did in the past—often stopping mid-gallop on her way through the living room to chase her tail in circle after circle before continuing on to grab a colorful toy from her wicker basket. Sometimes I think she wonders whose tail has been following her all these years—or else she just likes to make me laugh. Her body has loosened up to a place where she no longer sleeps in a tiny, little ball when we snuggle together. Actually, she stretches out *so* much now that it makes me yearn for a king size bed! Her breathing is shallower and slower, and her heart stays steady more often than not, rather than racing with anxiety. Mine, too.

Java still reacts around other dogs sometimes, but the biggest change is that her reaction is nowhere near as powerful and explosive. Her recovery time from stressful situations is nothing like it used to be, and she's able to make smarter choices overall. It used to take her almost thirty minutes to come back to the planet after spotting a dog one hundred yards away, and now she sniffs the ground without reacting from ten to fifteen feet away. She's also started to whine and wag her tail when she sees other dogs, and is making wonderful choices to walk away from stressful situations or hold still and watch calmly, rather than lunging and carrying on. When visitors came over in the past, Java jumped six feet in the air, then ran around the house for half an hour. Now, she keeps her feet on the ground and wags her entire body—usually hitting herself in the face with her tail until she can't stand it anymore. Then, she runs and grabs a toy. She's still nervous with some new people, but then again, so am I.

Java's coat is glossy and shiny, and she carries her body in a completely different way than she used to—with better posture, balance and confidence. The days of choke chains and giving up on walks have long given way to laughing, smiling, and enjoying our time together on leash. She's still young, and we're still learning and growing, so it'll only get better with more time and patience.

Our level of communication has come to a beautiful place of love, respect, and understanding, and our bond is closer than I ever knew a human/animal bond could be. Java teaches me what food she likes best, and works very hard to get me to understand what she's trying to tell me. She's very patient with me. It's still not totally clear whether her heavy nudge on my leg means she'd like to stalk squirrels in the back yard or get under the covers, but at least we've narrowed it down to two.

I remember a time not very long ago when a bouncy, little Plott Hound puppy magically appeared in my life—disguised as an angel with a big chunky head, soulful, chestnut eyes, and a brown and tan tiger-striped, well-muscled body. As I fill up the last few pages of our story, Java is lying quietly beside me in the sun, and reminding me what a gift she is in my life. Tears of gratitude make their way from my heart to my throat, then gently flow out of my eyes. Their warmth touches my cheeks, and I smile.

The Universe always has a plan, but we sometimes pass up the opportunity because of fear. Throughout my process of becoming who I want to be, I've learned to trust the feeling in my heart, because that's where the real truth lies. Some say it's the hardest journey in a lifetime to travel those eighteen or so inches from your head to your heart. I say it's the most important.

So, it is my wish for you to be inspired enough to take the leap forward—to spread your wings fully, and stretch all the way from your heart to your dreams. And if you're lucky enough to have an animal or human lying by your side right now, thank them, love them, and continue to learn and grow with them.

I double dog dare you.

Tag, you're it!

THE TAIL END

There were many times throughout the years where I felt frustrated, and even embarrassed and ashamed at times, for having a challenging and exuberant dog. Those moments became further and further apart as Java and I got grayer, wiser and more mellow.

As I look back, what floats to the top is immense gratitude for having spent so many amazing moments with such an outstanding dog. Java was one of a kind. I am forever grateful for all that she taught me, and for the multitude of gifts she gave so freely throughout her life and death.

She was a true example of living, aging and dying with dignity and grace - sharing her last breath and heartbeat with me while I held her gently in my arms and sang to her as she let go naturally at home.

There isn't a day that goes by that I don't think of her and smile from every cell in my body. I am blessed. It was by no mistake how our paths crossed on that wintry morning at the shelter back in 2001. Java is an angel in my life, and she continues to share her gifts from the other side. Where life leads me next, only the Universe knows, but I still have my sparkly, silver magic wand in the back pocket of my old, faded blue jeans—and a poop bag.

THE AUTHORS

Sage Lewis is the Creature Teacher™ with Dancing Porcupine LLC, and is a Certified Tellington TTouch® Advanced Practitioner for Companion Animals and People, Animal Communicator, Animal Hospice Consultant, Intuitive/Medium, Certified Life Coach & Shamanic Practitioner. She is the author of *JAVA: The True Story* and *Where Angels Play: Life, Death and The Magic Beyond*.

Java was an accomplished teacher, student, dancer, and warrior. She was an exuberant Plott Hound with the wisdom of a sage, and the spirit of a puppy. She was the dog who led Sage to where she is today, and vice versa. Java makes her home wherever she feels like it.

Sage continues to share her work in the world with both animals and people, and currently lives and plays in Prescott, AZ with her very creative husband, James, and their intelligent and loving dog, Reggae. Today, Sage and Reggae share their gifts together as a certified therapy team.

REGGAE 3/23/2015-?

FOR MORE INFORMATION
www.DancingPorcupine.com
Sage Lewis • 612-817-4473

TELLINGTON TTOUCH®

"We have so many incredible people,

in so many countries,

who are attracted to this work."

~ Linda Tellington-Jones

How does one explain this gentle and effective process of working with animals (and people) called Tellington TTouch® Training? When I first came across it years ago, I was drawn in because of the words 'gentle' and 'no fear or force.' After spending many years immersed in the work, I've come to realize that it's much more. When you see the results, there's no question about the incredible changes that take place from this gentle method of touch and movement.

By doing these circular TTouches, lifts and slides, animals and humans learn to understand in a new way, and increase their intelligence or ability to adapt to new situations. The TTouches affect the cells, nervous system and brain, and support better function and deeper learning. We also add various equipment and leading exercises to help create better balance and focus.

Animals also intensify their ability to stay centered and focused, rather than relying on old, habitual patterns. With a variety of informal studies, Tellington TTouch® has been found to have a measurable effect on brainwave patterns, most noticeably increasing the theta brainwave activation.

Simply put, Tellington TTouch® is a method of touch and movement which helps to relax a creature enough so they're able to think and make better choices. When we're relaxed, we can think more clearly and make healthier choices. The same is true for all beings.

www.TTouch.com

www.ingramcontent.com/pod-product-compliance
Lightning Source LLC
Chambersburg PA
CBHW061427040426
42450CB00007B/927